The Illustrated Guide to

DIVINATION

JUDY HALL

 A GODSFIELD BOOK

Library of Congress Cataloging-in-Publication
Data Available

10 9 8 7 6 5 4 3 2 1

Published in 2000 by
Sterling Publishing Company, Inc.
387 Park Avenue South, New York, N.Y. 10016
© 2000 Godsfield Press
Text © 2000 Judy Hall

Judy Hall asserts the moral right to
be identified as the author of this work.

Distributed in Canada by Sterling Publishing
c/o Canadian Manda Group, One Atlantic Avenue, Suite 105, Toronto, Ontario, Canada M6K 3E7
Distributed in Australia by Capricorn Link (Australia) Pty Ltd, P O. Box 6651, Baulkham Hills, Business Centre, NSW 2153, Australia

Every effort has been made to ensure that all the information
in this book is accurate. However, due to differing conditions, tools, and individual skills, the publisher cannot be
responsible for any injuries, losses, and other
damages which may result from the use
of the information in this book.

Designed for Godsfield Press by
The Bridgewater Book Company
Photographer Ian Parsons
Illustrator Ivan Hissey
Picture researcher Polly High

Printed and bound in China

ISBN 0–8069–2775–5

Acknowledgments
The publishers would like to thank the following for the use of pictures:
Adrian Bentley p 113
The Bridgeman Art Library: pp 6, 7, 10, 11, 12–13, 20, 34, 39, 40, 61, 107, 115
Corbis: pp 56, 58
e.t.archive: pp 7, 60
Fortean Picture Library: pp 34, 50,
Images Colour Library: pp 9, 21, 60, 68
Mary Evans Picture Library: pp 77, 98
Rachel Bean: pp 21, 95, 102,
Thema GmbH: p 69
Tony Stone Images: pp 51, 54
Werner Forman Archive: p 62

Special thanks to
A Ferguson and K Newton for help with photography

Special thanks for help with properties to
AGMüller, Neuhasen, Switzerland for permission to reproduce Swiss Tarot cards
Carta Mundi (Belgium) for permission to reproduce Tarot de Marseilles cards
Dice & Games Limited, Sudbury, Suffolk, UK for the photograph of Astro dice

The Illustrated Guide to

DIVINATION

Contents

AUTHOR NOTE: *The Tarot spreads used throughout this book are examples only.*

An Ancient Art

Stones have been known to move and trees to speak
Augers and understood relations have
By maggot-pies and choughs and rooks brought forth
SHAKESPEARE: MACBETH

Prophecy and divination have been used for thousands of years. Soothsayers, shamans, oracles, sorcerers, rune masters, prophets, and priests all sought to interpret divine will and predict what was to come.

ANCIENT TRADITIONS

In Greece the oak leaves at Dodona whispered their secrets to the priests at least 4,500 years ago. Celts and Druids honored the prophetic power of trees. But the tradition went far back into prehistory when ancient shamans listened to secrets carried on the wind.

A wild disheveled figure chewing hallucinogenic leaves, surrounded by smoke, and muttering incomprehensively, the Pythia at Delphi was a typical oracle of her time. But drugs have been used for prophecy since time immemorial. The Roman soothsayer poking around in bloody entrails and warning Caesar to beware the Ides of March was also following a long tradition. Such a soothsayer was kin to Aboriginal and Indian medicine men, the African witchdoctor, and the Siberian shaman.

Systems of divination mentioned in the Bible include witchcraft, astrology, casting lots, hepatoscopy (inspecting the liver of a sacrificed animal), oniromancy (dream interpretation), necromancy (raising the dead), rhabdomancy (rod or wand dowsing), consulting the teraphim (household gods), and "reading" air, fire, water, thunder, lightning, and meteors. In Egypt strange, distorted voices boomed out from statues of gods to predict events. If esoteric tradition is correct, Tarot cards originated in ancient Egypt, and this magical land was full of omens and portents. Several Egyptian oracles still exist and the symbology is just as powerful today.

This Loango Coast magician carries on a centuries old African tradition of "reading the bones" and other divinatory techniques. He is a much respected member of his community, just as his ancestors were.

This Burne-Jones painting depicts the ancient art of scrying or crystal gazing.

Nostradamus was consulted by the Queen of France with regard to the fate of her family – a fate he was able to predict accurately. But his success put him in danger of religious persecution.

In ancient China sticks were thrown for guidance and insight, a practice that was followed all over the ancient world. Crystal balls were scryed (gazed into), dice thrown, and cards laid. Animals and birds were augurs. Anything and everything could foretell the future.

The medieval seer and astrologer carried forward knowledge that was at least five thousand years old. Figures such as Nostradamus drew on this ancient tradition to make predictions that stretched far into the future. Nostradamus used both astrology and scrying to pierce the veil of the future and his work attracted the attention of the then Queen of France. But Nostradamus lived in fear of persecution and his predictions were carefully encoded into a series of enigmatic quatrains, which are open to several interpretations. His oracular book *Centuries* has been continuously in print for longer than any other book except the Bible.

In England, the Tudor queens Mary and Elizabeth were advised on matters of government by the seer Dr. John Dee, who employed astrology, geomancy, and a black obsidian ball.

Modern-Day Usage

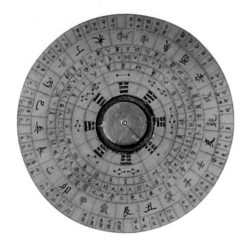

No one can be absolutely sure of the future, but we can support people to make the best of their present choices and opportunities so that the future can be as healthy and happy as possible.

DAVID LAWSON: PSYCHIC POTENTIAL

Today many people read "their stars," the daily horoscope in newspapers and magazines. Even the most skeptical will quickly glance at what is in store – and most probably promptly forget it unless it is dead on. But there is much more to oracles and divination than this (and more to astrology too).

The I Ching embodies the ancient wisdom of the East and is still popular today.

THE ROOTS OF DIVINATION

In all divination there is a core activity: Accessing knowledge beyond everyday reality. To do this many tools are used: Cards, dice, crystals, sticks, and stones to name but a few. They may appear to have nothing to do with each other, but most have their roots in a past tradition that they share, at least by intent. What is common to all methods of divination is the use of insight or intuition to gain information that would not otherwise be accessible and the belief that divination is a sacred act: That is, that this knowledge comes from the divine.

The I Ching traditionally used yarrow sticks to construct the hexagrams – nowadays coins are often used.

MODERN-DAY PRACTICE

While all systems of divination follow an ancient tradition, this is perhaps the first time in history when so many different methods have been widely available around the world. Oracles from China and Japan rub shoulders with the Native American tradition, with ancient Egyptian and British systems of divination, and with omens and augurs of every kind from all corners of the globe. At least three types of astrology are practiced worldwide: Western, Vedic, and Chinese. All have been in existence for thousands of years, yet still have relevance to the modern world.

Horoscope columns
in magazines give
you a glimpse into
the possibilities that
astrology offers.
A detailed reading
takes you much further.

*I Ching readers carry
out their task using texts
that have been passed
down for millennia*

Such traditions are no longer secret, known only to a few initiates. There are more professional readers and seers than at any time in history. In Britain, Australia, and most of North America you can have your palm read, consult the Tarot cards or an astrologer, or watch someone gaze into a crystal ball on your behalf without fear of prosecution or persecution. On the other hand, with the enormous number of divination packs available, everyone can now learn to divine for themselves, to consult an oracle, or tune into their own inner guidance. Tarot packs proliferate. New systems of divination are coming on to the market every week, and old ones are revived or presented in a fresh way. With a little guidance you too can access your future.

HELPING YOURSELF

There are divination packs and oracles for just about every purpose you can envisage. If you want to understand what is happening in your life, know more about your direction, examine choices you are faced with, or gain insight into why you seem blocked in your ambitions, there are tools to help you. If you want to understand your dreams, the way is open. If you want to know the celestial influences that you are under, or the subconscious forces that motivate you, you can discern these in the pages that follow.

If you want to comprehend yourself and your relationships better, or learn how to live more in harmony with other people, you can identify an appropriate method. If you seek spiritual understanding and insight, or to reach psychological enlightenment, help is at hand. If expanding your creativity is your aim, cards can help you. If you simply want to have some fun, even this is available – although you may be surprised to find how accurate even a lighthearted reading can be.

*Crystal balls can offer a
glimpse into the past or the
future, the choice is yours.*

What Oracles Do

For I dipt into the future, far as human eye could see
Saw the Vision of the world, and all the wonder that would be
Saw the heavens fill with commerce, argosies of magic sails
Pilots of the purple twilight, dropping down with costly bales
Heard the heavens fill with shouting, and there rain'd a ghastly dew
From the nations airy navies grappling in the central blue

ALFRED LORD TENNYSON 1809–1892

Divination offers guidance, it does not tell you what to do. It points to choices and possibilities. Oracles can warn of impending events and show you a way to steer through these, but an oracle cannot show you how to avoid them. Used wisely, oracles help you to know yourself.

WHAT IS DIVINATION?

Divination is ascertaining the future through insight or intuition. In the poem quoted above, Tennyson foresees war in the skies, even though he is writing in 1842, over seventy years before a plane flew, and bombs and chemical warfare became a reality. Yet he saw "costly bales" and "ghastly dew" carried by "airy navies." His poetic muse took him forward into the future.

"Oracle" comes from the Latin word *orare*, which means to pray or to speak. The role of Oracles is to act as intermediaries between the gods and humankind, so an oracle is a divine communication. Divination tools provide a focus for extrasensory perception. The images used are archetypes, evocative symbols that speak to the intuitive mind.

Divination is often seen as discerning a fixed and preordained future. However, there has always been a dialogue between "fate" and "free

The Greek sun-god Apollo had many shrines dedicated to him. He was believed to speak through his oracles, human or otherwise. The fate of nations often hung on his words as rulers consulted his priests for guidance before taking action.

will." In ancient eyes, "fate" was the will of the divine, but it could change at any moment. This was why offerings were made to propitiate the gods – especially before consulting the oracle!

FATE VERSUS FREE WILL

The doctrine of "fate" says that everything is pre-ordained. Each person has a plan laid down for them from which they cannot deviate. So, the Roman chronicler Plutarch in his biography of Julius Caesar tells us that:

A certain soothsayer forewarned him of a great danger which threatened him on the Ides of March and when the day was come, as he was going to the senate house, Caesar called to the soothsayer and said, laughing: "The Ides of March are come," to which the soothsayer answered "Yes, but they are not yet gone."

And, of course, by the end of the day Julius Caesar was dead. This was his fate. There are those who say, however, that had he heeded the warning, he could have avoided that fate.

The doctrine of "free will" says that everyone has the power to direct their own actions voluntarily. It offers opportunities for growth and change. The choices you make, the decisions you avoid, carve out your destiny.

Although these two approaches seem mutually incompatible, they can be reconciled. There is a path marked out – by yourself or your god. Some would call this "karma" (the result of past actions). How you approach this path depends on how you exercise your free will, whether you blindly follow the dictates of fate or seek to grow wiser through the choices you make.

KNOWING YOURSELF

Over the entrance to the Oracle at Delphi was carved "Know Thyself." While many modern-day oracles and divination tools purport to act as intermediaries between you and your fate, others help you to know yourself better. If you understand the hidden parts of your nature, the fears and desires that subconsciously drive you, then you have more control over your future.

If Caesar had heeded the warning to beware the Ides of March he could have avoided the unkindest cut of all.

Choosing an Oracle

First make up your mind, then consult the oracles.

MO TSE

There is hunger for insight and guidance. People want to know what the future holds for them. Will ancient predictions come to pass? How will life change? What will the personal effect be? And the spiritual? In olden times, you would consult the oracle, the astrologer, or the caster of runes. Today, there are many methods of foreseeing the future to choose from.

CONSULTING THE ORACLE

Years ago, the ability to read the future was an art known only to a few. But times have changed. While you can still consult a professional reader, there is an enormous number of self-help systems of divination. Each system of divination has much to offer. But finding exactly the right system can be difficult. You know you need an oracle, but which one?

Much money can rest on the throw of a die but Lady Luck can also advise those who consult her on other matters.

HOW TO USE THIS BOOK

This book is a comprehensive introduction to different systems of divination. If you wish to interpret a symbol or an "omen" such as a dream or an animal crossing your path, then you can look up the meaning within these pages. If you want to know what a card or dice number means, it is here. So too is guidance on reading a crystal ball or using dowsing. You will find not only introductions to "oracle"-type pronouncements, but also guides to psychological and spiritual insight that help you to grow at a deeper level, and move forward in your life in a new way.

CHOOSING A SYSTEM

You can choose your divination tool in one of two ways. First, you may glance through the book to see which illustrations catch your eye. If you are strongly drawn toward a particular illustration or symbol, this system will work for you. Secondly, you can carefully formulate your question (see page 18). Then look to see whether it is a straightforward "predictive" question – such as: "Will I get the job?" – or whether

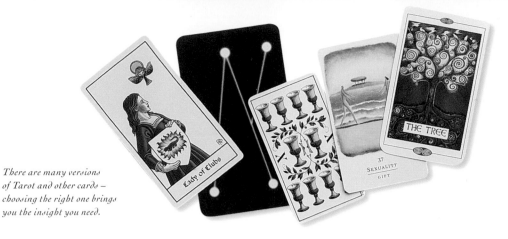

There are many versions of Tarot and other cards – choosing the right one brings you the insight you need.

it has emotional, psychological, or spiritual significance. This helps you to choose an oracle, since you will discover different systems are better suited to different kinds of question.

FOCUSING ON THE QUESTION

The question: "Will I find the right relationship soon?" could be asked at various levels. You may want only a yes or no answer. In that case dowsing could be sufficient. A crystal oracle could also have something to say. Because timing is involved, astrology could provide an answer. A Tarot reading could set out the timing and any obstacles in your path.

But, the question could be either emotional or psychological. Some of the newer Tarot card packs or the specially designed self-awareness systems would be appropriate. These would tell you the inner changes you need to put in place to attract exactly the right relationship. They would also pinpoint the

Astrology is a useful divination system if you need to know about timing and trends in addition to gaining insight into character and compatibility.

emotional basis on which you asked the question in the first place – does it arise out of the need simply to fill a hole in your life, to make yourself feel wanted or complete, or does it arise out of a desire for a life-enhancing partnership?

GETTING TO KNOW YOUR ORACLE

You can use your oracle in a "getting to know you, getting to know me" way. The more you understand the oracle, the more authentic will be your use of it, and the deeper the wisdom and insights you access when using it. So, if you practice with your oracle, choosing one card or symbol to work with for a few days at a time and meditating on it to allow the meaning to rise up into your consciousness, when you come to do a reading you will have a much wider range of possible meanings than if you only look the meaning up in a book.

A WORD OF WARNING

It has become something of a tradition that Tarot packs are stolen rather than paid for. This is because it is believed to be better to acquire a pack rather than buy it. However, stealing imbues a pack with negative vibrations and attracts karma. If you do not wish to purchase a pack, then ask for one as a gift.

A pendulum is particularly useful for quickly answering "yes/no" and "where" questions but it can point to deeper matters too.

Caring for Your Oracle

Some experts recommend somewhat precious and esoteric handling
for your Tarot deck, but such care is mostly common sense.

CAITLIN MATTHEWS: CELTIC WISDOM

*Many oracles today are available prepackaged but they can be placed in specially made bags or cloths. Storing
your oracle in a safe place prevents it from picking up other people's vibrations and keeps it attuned to your own.
Appropriate care of your oracle includes cleansing negative vibrations and creating a safe space in which to read.*

*Choose a beautiful
box or bag to keep
your treasured oracle
safe and free from
other people's vibes.*

STORING YOUR ORACLE

The thought of a friend casually picking up a pack
and riffling through it would have horrified the
seers of old. Oracles were secret, personal, and
sacred. They were usually carried in a pouch
secreted somewhere about the person. Rarely
were they put on open display. If the oracle was a
living being – a tree or a person for example – it
was approached with all due ceremony and honor.

It is an esoteric tradition that only the owner
handles an oracle, be it cards, crystals, or runes.
Readers may hand cards or runes to their clients
to shuffle or select so that their vibrations
impregnate the oracle, but the oracles are kept
carefully wrapped between sessions and are never
loaned to others.

Many of the divination packs available today
come with pouches or bags in which to keep
them. If they do not, you can make your own or
use a scarf to wrap them. Traditionally bags were
of silk, velvet, or leather; wooden boxes were also

favored. Natural fibers are believed to keep the vibrations pure. When you have completed a card reading, returning the cards to their original order breaks their contact with the question you have just been asking. According to Chinese custom, the I Ching should be kept above shoulder height.

CLEANSING ORACLES

Oracles can quickly pick up the vibrations of the user, the sitter, or the passer-by. Some systems of divination utilize this ability. But once this has happened, then the vibrations need to be cleared; and oracles are kept wrapped when not in use to prevent them from picking up unwanted or polluting vibrations. Whether you use your oracle to read for yourself or for other people, it will need cleansing from time to time. "Smudging" is a time-honored way of cleansing the vibrations. The divination aid is passed through the smoke of burning sage, sweetgrass, or incense. Crystals are traditionally cleansed with water, salt, and sun

but they, and other divination aids, can be cleansed instantly with essences such as Crystal Clear, which are made for this purpose.

CREATING A SAFE SPACE

A safe space is somewhere sacred, protected, and suitable for its purpose. Many people like to start their divinatory activities with a prayer for divine guidance. Setting up a safe space is easy. A simple meditation will create the right atmosphere. Close your eyes, concentrate for a moment and picture a ball of light in the center of the space in which you are going to do the reading. Let the light grow to fill the whole space, cleansing and protecting as it goes. If there is a need for more protection, a green pyramid is useful. Picture yourself in the center of the pyramid, with four sides around you meeting above your head, and a floor under your feet. You can use light to sweep out the pyramid both before you start and when you have completed the reading.

A smudge stick is an old way of cleansing the vibes from an oracle. Pass the oracle through its smoke.

Regular cleansing of crystals is essential if they are to show you the way forward. Visualizing light around your crystal is an excellent way to cleanse it.

Setting Out Your Oracle

© Carta Mundi

CAVALIER DE BATON
THE KNIGHT OF CLUBS

Casting a spread and conducting a reading can bring
an extraordinary level of clarity, awareness, and illumination.

DAVID LAWSON: THE EYE OF HORUS

There are many different spreads for setting out your oracle. Some are used purely for that particular oracle, others can be applied to several oracles. When choosing a spread, relate it to your question. It is a waste of effort to ask a "when" question of a spread that does not give timings, or a "why" question of a spread that does not go deeply into the background of a situation as well as what will happen in the future.

If you are using cards, be sure to shuffle them well before laying out. It is possible to deliberately reverse cards or to swirl them around on the table first. Oracles should be laid out in the order indicated by the numbering on the diagram for the spread. If a significator is called for, this can be chosen beforehand or selected at random by how the oracle falls.

Year Ahead

1
Month 1
(current)

11
One years
time

2

10

3

4

9

5
Six months
time

8

6

7

Three Card Spread

1
Past

2
Present

3
Future

THREE SPREAD

This very simple spread graphically sets out the past, present, and future. It can be read at different levels according to the question and the depth of insight required.

YEAR AHEAD

This spread shows the current influences and what will be coming into play over the next twelve months. It is useful as a general, overall view and can offer timings.

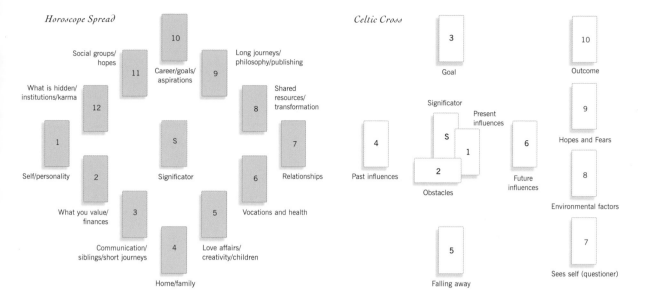

Horoscope Spread

- 10 — Career/goals/aspirations
- 11 — Social groups/hopes
- 9 — Long journeys/philosophy/publishing
- 12 — What is hidden/institutions/karma
- 8 — Shared resources/transformation
- 1 — Self/personality
- S — Significator
- 7 — Relationships
- 2 — What you value/finances
- 6 — Vocations and health
- 3 — Communication/siblings/short journeys
- 5 — Love affairs/creativity/children
- 4 — Home/family

Celtic Cross

- 3 — Goal
- Significator
- S — Present influences
- 1
- 4 — Past influences
- 2 — Obstacles
- 6 — Future influences
- 5 — Falling away
- 10 — Outcome
- 9 — Hopes and Fears
- 8 — Environmental factors
- 7 — Sees self (questioner)

HOROSCOPE SPREAD

Based on the Twelve Houses of the Zodiac, this spread covers all areas of life and reveals the larger pattern. It pinpoints potential, illuminates character, and can point to relationship or career issues.

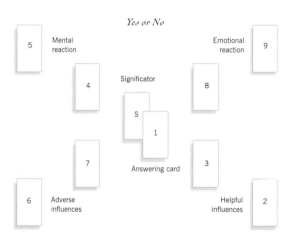

Yes or No

- 5 — Mental reaction
- 9 — Emotional reaction
- 4
- Significator
- 8
- S
- 1
- 7
- Answering card
- 3
- 6 — Adverse influences
- 2
- Helpful influences

YES OR NO?

This spread is designed to give a definite answer and to show the influences that surround the question. The question must need a "yes" answer or a "no" answer. An upright card in position one is a positive answer, a reversed one negative. Intellectual reactions show what the questioner thinks about the situation, emotional ones what is felt about it. Adverse influences show forces that may be acting against a successful outcome while helpful influences show what supports it.

CELTIC CROSS

One of the most general and non-specific layouts, the Celtic Cross is suitable for many oracles. The spread shows the history behind the question, present influences, obstacles to be overcome, environmental factors, and the possible future outcome. It is said to have a validity of three months – backward or forward. Questions of longer duration may need a different spread, although it can be surprisingly accurate when evaluating the outcome of a long-term goal.

GYPSY SPREAD

A classic spread for card reading, the Gypsy Spread can be used with other oracles too. It reveals past and present influences, both hidden and visible, and brings out the potential in a situation. Use this spread if you want to know what lies behind a situation, as well as looking forward, or to give an indication of timing.

- 1 | 2 | 3 — The self and what is awakening
- 4 | 5 | 6 — The environment and relationships
- 7 | 8 | 9 — Hopes, fears, and wishes
- 10 | 11 | 12 — What you expect
- 13 | 14 | 15 — Destiny and hidden influences
- 16 | 17 | 18 — The near future (2–3 months)
- 19 | 20 | 21 — The further future (4–6 months)

Gypsy Spread

Framing a Question

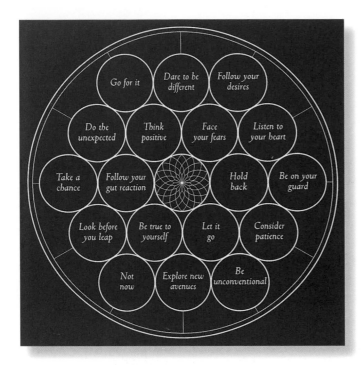

Go for it

Dare to be different

Follow your desires

Do the unexpected

Think positive

Face your fears

Listen to your heart

Take a chance

Follow your gut reaction

Hold back

Be on your guard

Look before you leap

Be true to yourself

Let it go

Consider patience

Not now

Explore new avenues

Be unconventional

I have answered three questions
and that is enough.

LEWIS CARROLL

Exactly what kind of question you ask, and how you phrase it, affects how accurate an answer is, as does your view of oracles. If you believe in fixed fate, that is what you will see. If you believe the future is flexible, you will see possibilities.
The oracle's answers could be open to different interpretations.

Consider your question carefully before throwing crystals for succinct advice.

QUESTIONING

Oracle answers are notoriously ambiguous. When Croesus asked the Delphic Oracle if he should make war on the Persians, he was told he would overthrow a great empire. He went to war; but it was his own empire that fell.

The type of question you ask will, to a large extent, determine how helpful the reply will be. Open questions create a space for something new to emerge, for the unseen to become visible. Open questions bring out potentials, illuminate choices, and highlight hidden resistance. Open questions allow and facilitate. Closed questions demand rigid yes-or-no answers – but few oracles give yes-or-no replies. Guidance is difficult to obtain from a closed question. "Wooly questions" are also hard to answer. Try to be succinct, and ensure the question is precisely framed.

If you make your question too simple, it may defeat itself. If it is too complex, you may have to stretch the answer to fit. Too many questions and the oracle refuses to answer. It is better to take questions in manageable chunks and do a reading in several parts with an appropriate oracle for each part. If you are trying to answer a complex psychological question, The Enlightenment Pack points with great accuracy to the lifescripts underlying events. If you want a simple answer, the Insight Wheel from The Crystal Wisdom Kit has answers such as "Hold back" or "Go for it."

Cards like The Enlightenment Pack have been specially formulated to bring you deep psychological insights.

Questions such as: "Why did he do that?" or "Will she marry me?" put the focus on the other person. Such questions not only block insights into your own self but also tend to receive answers that are easily misinterpreted. Readings that rely on someone else doing what the reading says they will do invariably disappoint.

OPEN ANSWERS

When you receive an answer, you may need to remain open to possibilities. An answer that seems to indicate one thing may actually point to something different. So, for instance, a woman's aunt was very ill. She had already made the 400-mile round trip several times to visit her. The hospital rang again saying her aunt had deteriorated. Wanting to be with her aunt when she died, she asked the oracle whether it would be appropriate to go. Opening a book at random, there was one sentence on the page: "There really is nothing left for her to do." She interpreted this to mean she should make the journey. She rang the hospital to say she was on her way only to be told her aunt had died as she was reading the oracle. There was nothing left to do.

Answers can be interpreted at different levels. If you asked if you were pregnant, for example, you could receive the answer: "Yes." This reply could, however, relate not to physical pregnancy but to the fact that you were pregnant in the sense that something was being gestated within you – a new possibility, a creative project, and so on. You would give birth in due time, but it would not be to a child.

THE WAY TO APPROACH THE ORACLE

So, for clear questions and answers focus on yourself. Ask precise, open questions – and not too many of them – and seek understanding and clarity rather than rigid answers. Write your questions down. Ponder them, take time to ensure that they are correctly phrased. Then ask the oracle.

USEFUL QUESTIONS

Please give me insight into ... ... (be precise)

How can I move forward?

What lies behind this situation?

What can I learn from this?

How is the past affecting the present?

Please clarify this situation for me. (set out the situation first)

Please show me how to resolve this situation.

What is needed to heal this situation?

Please reveal what is hidden from me in this situation.

Please give me guidance as to whether I should... (be precise)

What would be a good course of action for me?

What would be the result of this action? (specify action)

What would be the result of embarking on this relationship?

Eastern Oracles

Confucius based his philosophical system on the wisdom of the I Ching.

The ancient Chinese mind contemplates the cosmos in a way comparable to that of the modern physicist, who cannot deny that his model of the world is a decidedly psychophysical structure.

CARL GUSTAV JUNG

The Chinese I Ching has been in existence for at least five thousand years, Mah Jongg for over two thousand. Both have an oracular function. Zen Koans come from the spiritual teachings of Zen Buddhism and offer spiritual illumination.

CHINESE ORACLES

In ancient Chinese temples, yarrow sticks were cast to ascertain the future. These evolved into a complicated system of divination and self-understanding, the I Ching or *Book of Changes*. Two major philosophical systems, Confucianism and Taoism, have their roots in the I Ching. Chinese astrologers charted the progress of the planets by a divining board, Mah Jongg, which developed into a game. It is the ancestor of games such as ludo, dominoes, and Monopoly. However, Mah Jongg retained its sacred foundations and its rituals remind the player of its oracular nature. The tiles build a celestial map.

The original *Book of Changes* set out linear marks. A straight, unbroken line indicated "yes" and a broken line "no." Greater subtlety was gained from combining lines into pairs, and a third line was added to give eight basic trigrams. The trigrams combined to form sixty-four hexagrams. As with Mah Jongg these hexagrams described heaven and earth and all that happened within them. Everything was in a constant state of flux and transition, one thing dissolved or developed into another. Change was natural and the symbols are transitional states.

Fundamental to ancient Chinese understanding was the concept of Yin and Yang. Yin is passive, reflective, accepting, dark, and female. Yang is outgoing, active, initiating, bright, and male. The two are not opposites, they are different but complementary ends of a unity. One cannot exist without the other.

This tenth-century block book sets out the unchanging wisdom of the I Ching, carefully handed down since time immemorial.

A JAPANESE ORACLE

Buddhism reached Japan from China in the twelfth century CE where it acquired the name "Zen." It was taught by "koans," short pithy sentences of seeming paradoxes and confabulations which, when reflected upon, brought great insight into life. These have been translated into a modern oracle that can be used as a spiritual practice or for everyday insights.

WHAT EASTERN ORACLES CAN DO FOR YOU

Eastern oracles are subtle, and sometimes apparently inscrutable. They can highlight events and forces behind the visible façade of a situation. Both Chinese systems offer timings and insights within different layers of meaning. Zen Koans bring about spiritual enlightenment through a shift in perspective.

Traditionally, the I Ching was consulted using forty-nine yarrow sticks, while burning a ritual candle.

The I Ching

The I Ching is much more than a book of fortunes.
It is a complex system with universal laws governing the sixty-four hexagrams.

THROWING THE STICKS

The traditional method of consulting the I Ching uses forty-nine yarrow stalks and is extremely complicated. It is easier to use coins to obtain hexagrams. If you do not have traditional Chinese coins, use three coins of equal value – the side giving the value ("tails") is taken as inscribed and "heads" is blank. Shake the three coins in your hands, while concentrating on the question, and then throw.

MODERN COIN HEXAGRAMS

Three heads form an "Old Yang" line

Three tails form an "Old Yin" line

Two tails and one head form a "Young Yin" line

Two heads and one tail form a "Young Yang" line

USING THE I CHING

The first throw of the coins gives the bottom line of the hexagram. The coins are thrown a total of six times and the six lines of the hexagram are built up from the bottom line.

Because the hexagrams do not have "o" or "x" in them, both Old and Young Yang lines are first counted as Yang — , and both Old and Young Yin lines are counted as Yin − −. The text for the appropriate hexagram is then consulted.

If the initial reading gave no Old Yin or Yang lines, the reading is now at an end. If, however, Old Yin and Yang lines came up in the original hexagram, these are now said to change into their opposite, that is the Old Yang line becomes a Young Yin line, and the Old Yin line becomes a Young Yang line. This yields a second hexagram that is also consulted. It gives insight into the question at a deeper level or later on in time – "what will happen next."

THE VISUAL I CHING

To save complicated throws, hexagram forming, and Ritual Number assimilation, the Visual I Ching has hexagrams printed on sixty-four illustrated cards. It makes consulting the I Ching much simpler, but a more comprehensive book may be needed to recapture the subtlety and breadth of meaning in the *Book of Changes*.

TIMING

The Chinese use a lunar year. Each month has five hexagrams, each governing six days, so each line governs a day. Without a Chinese calendar it is difficult to ascertain precise timings but aligning February with the first month of the Chinese year gives an approximation (see table opposite).

1 Creativity
Progress steadfastly for success

2 Receptivity
Success comes through receptive perseverance

3 Difficulty
Success comes after initial difficulties

4 Youthful Folly
Learn slowly and listen to advice

5 Quiet Waiting
Wait until the time is right

6 Conflict
Obstacles to be overcome, avoid arguments

7 The Army
Time to fight in the company of others

8 Union
A peaceful and harmonious time

9 Gentle Power
Restraint during hard times

10 Conduct
Remain resolute

11 Peace
Share good fortune with others

12 Stagnation
A time of standstill, awaiting action

13 Brotherhood
Share your new success with others

14 Abundance
Combine study and work

15 Modesty
Be modest and accept help from others

16 Enthusiasm
Promote yourself without arrogance

17 Following
Go with the flow

18 Decay
Put right what has gone wrong

19 Approach
Advance cautiously and be magnanimous

20 Contemplation
Be on the alert

21 Gnaw Through
Stress your positive achievements

22 Grace
Cultivate the appearance of success

23 Splitting Off
Let go of an aspect of life that no longer serves

24 Turning Point
Change of seasons brings renewal

25 The Unexpected
Stay within limitations, use divine guidance

26 Persistence
Work hard and progress slowly

27 Nourishment
Watch and wait

28 Excess
Do not take on too much

29 The Abyss
Wait for a better time

30 Brightness
Use intellect and logic

31 Attraction
Do not envy others

32 Endurance
Allow things to take their course

33 Retreat
Others may try to take advantage

34 Power of the Great
Do not make empty threats

35 Progress
An improvement is at hand

36 Darkening of the Light
Remain centered during difficult times

37 The Family
The emphasis is on the home and duty

38 Opposition
Remain flexible

39 Obstruction
Go around obstacles where possible

40 Release
Things come to a head and move forward

41 Decrease
A time of scanty resources

42 Increase
A time of good fortune

43 Resolution
Legal action or insurance called for

44 Contact
Avoid the influence of others

45 Assembling
Meet opposition by going with the group

46 Ascending
Move steadily onward and upward

47 Oppression
Find strength in adversity

48 The Well
Do whatever has to be done, retain credit

49 Revolution
Others begin to see you as more impressive

50 The Cauldron
Service equipment and avoid major accidents

51 Thunder
Prepare for stormy weather

52 Stillness
Progress slowly and avoid unnecessary risks

53 Development
Progress slowly, if not imperceptibly

54 Marriageable Maiden
Do not demand too much, wait

55 Fullness
Inner happiness meets obstacles calmly

56 The Wanderer
Travel may be appropriate

57 Willing Submission
Bend with the wind for the time being

58 Joy
Inner contentment generates peace

59 Dissolution
Remain flexible and reasonable

60 Limitation
Build up your reserves

61 Inner Truth
Watch for the warning signs

62 Preponderance of the Small
Find a safe refuge, do small things

63 After Completion
Changing circumstances, consolidate gains

64 Before Completion
Make your cautious move at the right moment

TIMING

Date							Date						
First month (February)	11	5	17	35	40	51	Seventh month (August)	12	57	49	26	22	58
Second month (March)	34	16	6	18	45	51	Eighth month (September)	30	54	25	36	47	58
Third month (April)	43	56	7	8	9	51	Ninth month (October)	23	52	63	21	28	58
Fourth month (May)	1	14	37	48	31	20	Tenth month (November)	2	64	39	27	61	29
Fifth month (June)	44	50	55	59	10	20	Eleventh month (December)	24	3	15	38	46	29
Sixth month (July)	33	32	60	13	41	20	Twelfth month (January)	19	62	4	42	53	29

Mah Jongg

Mah Jongg is the art of Ya Pai Shen Po – divining by ivory blocks.

These Western Mah Jongg sets from the 1920s were based on much older traditional Chinese designs. The sets could be used for gaming or for divination.

THE TILES

A Mah Jongg set comprises 144 tiles with inscribed Chinese characters that can be used for divination. These have also been translated into modern cards. The set is made up of four identical decks of thirty-four cards, or tiles, plus eight "Guardians." The cards or tiles are divided into three suits – Bamboo, Circles, and Characters – and seven Honors, being the four Directions and three "Dragons."

The four Directions in Mah Jongg are actually an inversion of the earthly dimension. So, geographical East is West in Mah Jongg, and geographical North is South. This is because the directions form a map of the celestial heavens, not the Earth. As the Earth mirrors the heavens, the celestial sphere has reversed directions.

USING MAH JONGG

The Mah Jongg oracle is set out according to a precise, time-honored formula. Traditionally, it is orientated North–South and the diviner and the querent sit East–West, the querent taking the "East" position that is, geographically speaking, actually "West." You can also read the cards or tiles for yourself, and should occupy the E–W position to do this.

Having shuffled the tiles or cards, the reader pushes them all to the outside edges of the table, clearing the central area. Thirteen cards are drawn and placed face down in the center, making an "island within a lake." These thirteen are reshuffled. Three cards or tiles are placed to the "West" of the table. Three central cards or tiles are then drawn toward the "East," three

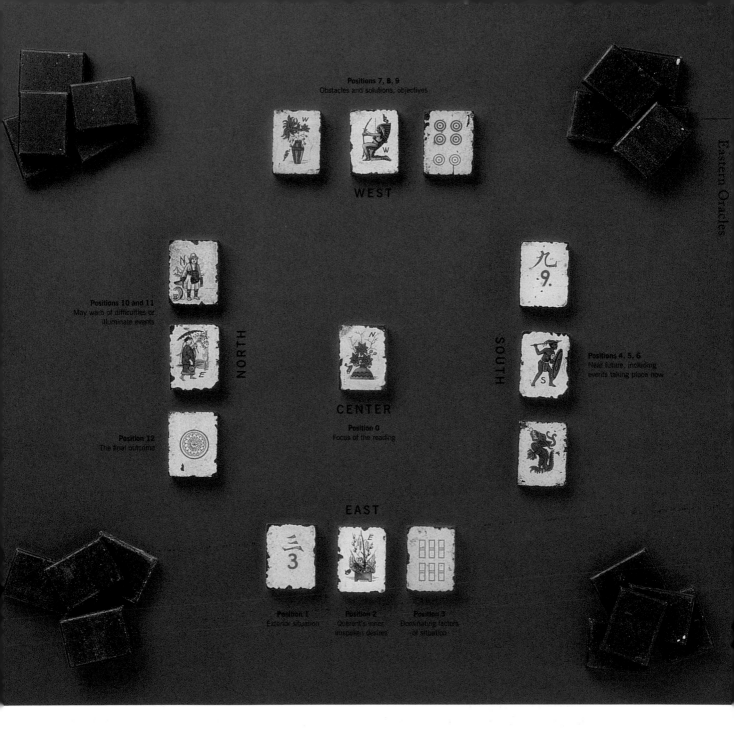

Positions 7, 8, 9
Obstacles and solutions, objectives

WEST

Positions 10 and 11
May warn of difficulties or
illuminate events

NORTH

SOUTH

Positions 4, 5, 6
Near future, including
events taking place now

Position 12
The final outcome

CENTER

Position 0
Focus of the reading

EAST

Position 1
Exterior situation

Position 2
Querent's inner,
unspoken desires

Position 3
Dominating factors
of situation

"North," and three "South," leaving one in the center (see layout guide). The cards or tiles are then turned over and read in sequence according to their specific meanings (the book accompanying *The Fortune Teller's Mah Jongg* has full details). If a Guardian has been selected, it is augmented by an additional card or tile from the outer edge of the table.

TIMING

The directions and the seasons traditionally associated with them in Mah Jongg point to timings: Spring is "East," Summer is "South," Autumn is "West," and Winter is "North." To time events, look to the current climatic season and see how far away the season represented by a card or tile is from the present.

Zen Koan

Koans come from the Zen Buddhist tradition. While they can help you to look at questions in your life, their main function is to help you to grow in spiritual insight, bringing about a different perspective. They teach you to be, rather than showing you what to do.

When setting out the Zen Koan cards, meditative spontaneity is more important than accuracy in the placing of the circle.

WHAT IS A KOAN?

Koans are "windows on Buddhism." Koan phrases are objects for contemplation, leading to deep insight into life. They may be illogical questions, paradoxes, or confabulations. They cast light on everyday life through the wisdom of Buddhist masters.

USING ZEN KOANS

Sit quietly, letting your mind become calm. Let your thoughts and feelings pass by rather than focusing on them. When you are ready, shuffle the koan cards. Arrange the cards in a circle in one continuous movement. Do not rearrange the circle. It is perfect as it is. The card circle allows you to focus on one of them and none of them (a very Zen thing to do!). The circle is an important Zen symbol of an empty, whole, enlightened mind. Creating a circle with the cards helps your mind to become empty of distractions, attentive, and ready to respond.

If you have a particular question, focus on it. If not, simply be open to what comes. Intuitively select a card. Read the koan, reflect on it, and allow your own spontaneous reaction to arise. Then consult the text for further meaning. Sit with your card, and view your question or situation from the new perspective. The meaning may be immediately clear or may take some time to make itself known.

Cards can be drawn daily or weekly as a spiritual practice. Your understanding of the card will deepen with a week's contemplation. Putting the card where it will catch your eye during the day helps you to attune. Each time you see it, repeat the koan, and allow room for new meaning to emerge.

THE KOANS

1 Who are you?
Recognize the Buddha nature.

2 To find yourself is to lose yourself.
Cease to identify with the
illusory separate self.

3 The wave and the sea are One.
Experience the depth of all things.

4 Look and see with your own eyes.
If you hesitate, you miss the mark forever.
Now is the only reality.

5 I burn the books in my bag.
But the verses written in my guts cannot
be forgotten. Express your true nature.

6 When walking – walk.
When sitting – sit. But don't wobble!
Do what you do with complete awareness.

7 Without anxious thought,
doing comes from being.
Free up the mind.

8 Do what you will –
but not because you must.
Lose old habits, be spontaneous.

9 Know who you are.
Be what you know.
See the truth and live authentically.

10 Water heats gradually and boils suddenly.
Awakening cannot be forced,
but it can be encouraged.

11 A mind is only absolutely pure when
it is above purity and impurity.
Be yourself – as you are.

12 The inner light is beyond praise and
blame. Like space it knows no boundaries.
The essential "I" experiences everything.

13 Don't search for Truth, simply stop
having opinions. Enlightenment is found
through the absence of opinions.

14 The Way is not difficult for
someone without preferences.
Completely accept what is.

15 Gaze at the stars but walk on the Earth.
Be practical and ordinary yet see
the miracle all around.

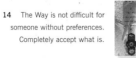

16 The wise don't strive to arrive.
Give up goal orientation and simply be.

17 With Zen, every day is a good day.
Without Zen, even good days are bad days.
Live without attachments.

18 Water is one essence: Drunk by a cow
it becomes milk, drunk by a snake it becomes
poison. Attitudes to life create experience of life.

19 The seeds of the past are the
fruits of the future. The law of karma.

20 We stand in our own shadow
and wonder why it is dark.
The problem lies in ourselves.

21 A weed is a treasure and a treasure is a weed.
By valuing some things and not others,
the value of everything is missed.

22 Make medicine from suffering.
Suffering is an opportunity
to awaken spiritually.

23 The fearless hero is a loving
child. True strength lies in
compassion and openness.

24 Great understanding comes
with great love. To be wise is to love,
to love is to be wise.

25 You smile – the world changes.
Love and joy are infectious.

26 The old pond.
A jumping frog – plop!
See the wonder of the present moment.

27 Immersed in water, you stretch
out your hands for a drink.
Appreciate the wonder of being alive.

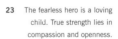

28 Grandfather dies, father dies, son dies –
this is good fortune. Know your deepest being
and live securely in a world of total insecurity.

29 While you are living, know you are dying.
Awareness of mortality
focuses the mind.

30 Mu! (Literal meaning: Not.)
There are no questions.

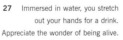

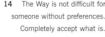

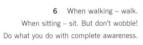

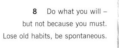

The Tarot

© Carta Mundi

The Tarot exerts a mysterious allure. Its accessible history is a tantalizing blend of slender facts and romantic speculation, while its symbols continue to have a powerful impact on everyone who sees them.

JANE LYLE: THE RENAISSANCE TAROT

The seventy-eight-card Tarot deck comprises fifty-six Minor Arcana cards, divided into four suits, and twenty-two pictorial cards known as the Major Arcana, or Trumps, and numbered from 0 to 21. The potent symbols of the Major Arcana stimulate intuition and allow access to archetypal information – universal knowledge. The cards can be laid out in a number of spreads, and the Major Arcana cards can be used alone.

ORIGINS

The Tarot cards are the forerunners of modern playing cards. Tarot suits of Cups, Wands, Pentacles, and Swords evolved into Hearts, Clubs, Diamonds, and Spades. Of the Major Arcana (trump) cards, only the Fool remains. He became the Joker.

The first Tarot cards appeared in the fourteenth century, a time of great religious persecution when esoteric ideas had to be encoded for safekeeping. The earliest complete extant deck was painted by Bonifacio Bembo early in the fifteenth century, placing the Tarot firmly against a Renaissance background. This deck, now in the Pierpoint Morgan Library in New York, is virtually identical to the modern Tarot deck.

The Joker arose out of the Tarot Fool card.

However, there is an esoteric tradition that says Tarot symbolism goes back to ancient Egypt and Rome. There appear to be links with Crusaders who had been in the East. The Saracens they fought had used cards for divination at least as early as the eighth century CE and the introduction of Tarot soon after the destruction of one of the most occult of the crusading orders, the Knights Templar, may have been no coincidence.

The cards shown here are examples from the Lovers' Tarot, Prediction Tarot, Enchanted Tarot, Renaissance Tarot, and Celtic Tarot.

MODERN TAROT

Nowadays there are over three hundred different Tarot packs available. Some rework the traditional symbols of the original Tarot, others introduce completely new elements, and there are packs that combine astrological and Tarot symbolism or elements of myth and fairy tale. The Tarot that will work for you is the one whose symbols resonate with your intuition. You may well find that you end up with several packs for different purposes. Virtually every pack comes with a detailed instruction book for interpretation.

WHAT TAROT CAN DO FOR YOU

Tarot is a complex system of divination. Its meanings are deep and subtle. The cards can be read at a superficial level for "fortune-telling" but they can also offer powerful insights into the forces operating both in your life and within your self. The Major Arcana can be taken as a journey of spiritual initiation.

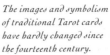

The images and symbolism of traditional Tarot cards have hardly changed since the fourteenth century.

Using Tarot

When you are ready to read the cards, sit down quietly and empty your mind of everything but the situation you are asking about. If you are using a cloth, spread it on the table in front of you.

LAYING OUT THE CARDS

There are many Tarot layouts. The most common spreads are shown in Setting out Your Oracle (pages 16–17), and timing methods are given below. Use two or three layouts for a question, because different spreads will throw light on different aspects of the situation. A "significator" to represent the questioner can be picked at random or chosen according to correspondences explained in your pack.

The most usual way to approach the cards is to shuffle the whole deck thoroughly while concentrating on the question. The pack is then cut into three and the piles placed face down in front of you. Pick up the last cut pile and place it on top of the first pile, then place the second pile on top of that. Deal the cards face down into the chosen spread. Alternatively, the cards can be fanned out after shuffling, and the number of cards needed for the spread picked out at random. As you read, turn the cards over. If you want to use only the Major Arcana, separate this before shuffling.

REVERSED CARDS

In Tarot reversed cards have a particular meaning. To obtain reverse cards you can either reverse some of the cards (without looking at them), or mix the pack around on the table.

TIMING

With the Tarot, the suits can correspond to seasons. While it is not always possible to time an event accurately, the cards can give you some indication. The timing spread in the next section is one method; another is to use the twos, threes, and fours from the Minor Arcana to represent months as shown:

TIMING			
Suit	**2**	**3**	**4**
Swords	March	April	May
Wands	June	July	August
Cups	September	October	November
Pentacles	December	January	February

(taken from Jane Lyle: Renaissance Tarot)

Count off thirteen cards from the top of the deck, stopping if the two, three, or four of any of the suits appears. This is the answer. If none of the cards appears, count off another thirteen cards. If a timing card still does not appear, the question may still be undecided. Any reply you receive is likely to be unreliable or there may be a delay in the outcome.

IV   EMPEROR   HEH ♑

♂ MARS   ARIES   SUN ☀

The Mandala Astrological pack
combines astrological symbolism
with that of traditional Tarot.

A TIMING "YES-NO" SPREAD

This spread uses the Aces to time events – Wands: spring; Cups: summer; Swords: autumn; Pentacles: winter (upright: early; reversed: late). It answers a clearly formulated question that requires a yes-or-no answer. The question should begin "Will I ... ?" and ask "When?"

Deal the cards face up before you in the first of three piles. Stop when you reach an Ace or when there are thirteen cards. Make all three piles in this way, working from right to left. Discard the remaining cards. An upright Ace is "yes," a reversed Ace "no." A reversed Ace or another reversed card in either of the first two piles can indicate that the question has not yet been resolved or can show the reason why things are not moving. Three reversed Aces indicate a categorical "no" and the piles can be read to see why not. No Aces means the matter is still undecided and again the piles can be read for deeper insight.

SPECIALIST PACKS

If your question is about a specific area of life, such as relationships, then there are Tarot packs that are designed specially. The Lovers' Tarot, for instance, focuses on love, sex, and relationships and explores doubts and fears as well as offering insight into urgent longings and desires. The Mandala Astrological Tarot is one of several packs that combine astrology with Tarot for deeper meaning. Other specialized Tarot packs appear under different headings throughout this book.

It is usual to lay
Tarot cards out on a
cloth kept specially
for the purpose.
This is the Celtic
Cross spread.

Major and Minor Arcana

© Carta Mundi

MAJOR ARCANA
The names of cards differ slightly in the various decks but the number remains the same.

0. The Fool
New Beginnings, Change
Reversed Folly

1. The Magician
Manifestation, Creative Action
Reversed Delay

2. The High Priestess
Wisdom, Intuitive Action
Reversed Ignorance

3. The Empress
Fertility, Achievement
Reversed Inaction

4. The Emperor
Worldly Power, Success
Reversed Loss of Authority

5. The Pope
Knowledge, Mentor
Reversed Unsound Advice

6. The Lovers
Choice, Relationship
Reversed Unreliability

7. The Chariot
Great Effort, Adversity
Reversed Overcome Defeat

8. Justice
Fairness, Justice
Reversed Bias

9. The Hermit
Wise Counsel, Discretion
Reversed Imprudence

10. The Wheel of Fortune
Destiny, Advancement
Reversed Reverses

11. Force
Endurance, Stronger Position
Reversed Weakness

12. The Hanged Man
Transition, Readjustments
Reversed Suspension

13. Death
Transformation, Great Change
Reversed Stagnation

14. Temperance
Balance, Compatibility
Reversed Discord

15. The Devil
Commitment, Material Power
Reversed Obsession

16. Lightning Struck Tower Challenge to Awake, Unexpected Events *Reversed* Chaos

17. The Star
Hope, Bright Future
Reversed Disappointment

18. The Moon
The Unconscious, Visions
Reversed Confusion

19. The Sun
Vitality, Success,
Reversed Loneliness

20. Judgment
Rebirth, New Directions
Reversed Delay

21. The World
Completion, Fulfillment
Reversed Resistance

MINOR ARCANA

The Minor Arcana is divided into four suits: Swords, Wands, Cups, and Pentacles. Wands may also be called "Rods" or "Staves," and Pentacles "Coins." Each suit goes from Ace (one) to ten with four "Court" cards, the King, Queen, Knight, and Page – some packs have a Prince and Princess. In a reading, Court cards can represent people or situations.`

THE SUITS

The suits indicate different aspects of daily life, challenges and opportunities that arise, and how these will be met.

Swords
Conflict and discord. At its best decisive action. Cutting to the heart of the matter, bringing clarity. Intellectual, associated with communication, decisions, and law. Dealing with mental aspect of daily life, may indicate state of mind rather than actual events.

Haircolor
Very dark- or gray-haired people

Wands
Fiery temperament, enterprise, creativity, and challenge. Travel in all its manifestations, deals, and negotiations of all kinds. Politics, property, family, and career aspects of daily life.

Haircolor
Brown-haired people

Cups
Romantic, heart-centered, love and happiness, eroticism, and affairs. Can indicate marriage and friendships. Abundance, personal possessions, and the arts. The emotional aspect of daily life.

Haircolor
Fair-haired people

Pentacles
The five senses, money, material possessions, and services. Status, home, and financial issues. Worldly concerns, ranging from routines of daily work to cleaning the house. Money and the material aspects of daily life.

Haircolor
Dark- or gray-haired people

For more detailed interpretations, see the book accompanying the Tarot pack of your choice.

MINOR ARCANA INDICATIONS

Ace of any suit
The start of something new according to the nature of the suit

Two of any suit
Partnership matters of all kinds

Three of any suit
New projects including joint enterprises

Four of any suit
Stability and security; how roots are put down

Five of any suit
Letting go of outworn attitudes; loss and regret

Six of any suit
Taking up challenges and moving forward

Seven of any suit
Working out priorities and values

Eight of any suit
Expanding horizons, new jobs or attitudes

Nine of any suit
Where you find satisfaction and security

Ten of any suit
Finding completion and the heart's desire or experiencing rejection

Page of any suit
Children or young women. Information

Knight of any suit
Young men. Movement forward and challenges

Queen of any suit
Mature women. Comfort, nurturing, and satisfaction

King of any suit
Mature men. Worldly success, achievements and assertion

Casting the Runes

Each rune is a pictorial representation
of a particular natural mood or condition.

JOHN TREMAINE: CASTING THE RUNES

Runes are an ancient, sacred, and symbolic alphabet from the Norse tradition. Used for all aspects of life, they were cast for fertility, protection, binding spells, and working rituals. Runes are traditionally fashioned from wood, or incised or painted onto suitable stones or clay tablets.

RUNECRAFT

Runecraft began several thousand years ago in Scandinavia. The word "rune" means secret writing and the letters were full of magical power. Symbols were carved on rocks to represent birds, animals, and other natural beings. Runic practice incorporated materials from the natural world, because such materials were believed to be imbued with sacred energy.

ODIN'S ENLIGHTENMENT

Runes were dedicated to the god Odin, associated with healing, travel, communication, and divination. Mythology tells us that, searching for enlightenment, Odin hung himself upside down on Yggdrasil, the World Tree, impaled upon his own spear for nine days. As he gazed at the ground, rune stones hidden among the roots of the tree revealed themselves.

As the Germanic tribes spread out across Europe, the runes traveled with them. By Roman times they had evolved into the Futhark, a runic alphabet. Interpretation was a mystery granted to a special few or conferred on the head of the

The Norse god Odin with his two crows Hugin (Thought) and Mumin (Memory).

household. In Anglo-Saxon England, kings and bishops had the power to read the runes but later the practice fell into disuse.

Runic symbols were traditionally incised upon small pieces of wood.

USING THE RUNES

Runes packs are available, but you can also make your own by painting them onto suitable smooth pebbles or incising them into pieces of wood or clay. Rune stones are best kept in a bag or pouch.

Before making your choice sit quietly holding the runes while you focus on your question. Then, after thorough shuffling, they can be tumbled out onto a cloth or pulled out from the bag to be laid in spreads.

WHAT RUNES CAN DO FOR YOU

Runes help you to look deep inside yourself. Pinpointing your innermost fears and desires, they highlight hidden factors that will create your future, and show you the choices that you face. Describing positive and negative influences, runes point out how you can overcome negativity and make constructive choices for the future.

This colorful Rune Stone from Skansen Park, Stockholm has been painted by archeologists to show what the stone would have looked like when it was new.

Rune Spreads

THE THREE-RUNE SPREAD

One of the easiest spreads uses three runes. The first rune pulled from the bag (or card taken from the pack) indicates the situation; the second, the action required; and the third reveals the outcome.

Rune cards are light and portable, easily slipped into the pocket ready for an impromptu consultation.

UPRIGHT OR REVERSED?

Nine of the runes read the same whichever way up they fall. The remainder look different depending on whether they are upright or reversed. The meaning is subtly changed by the way the stone falls (or card turns). In general, reversed stones (cards) point to negative situations or influences that need to be addressed, or to the necessity for caution. They often point to an aspect of yourself that you have been unwilling to face but are now ready to acknowledge.

YEAR AHEAD

If you need a timing, or wish to look at the year ahead, laying out the runes like the numbers on a clock gives you twelve months of the year. Either shuffle the cards and lay twelve out in a circle, or pull twelve stones from the bag. Each rune indicates a "theme" for that month.

Other layouts can be adapted from Tarot spreads.

Tactile Runes made from polished wood, like these from Janet Thompson's Rune Pack, are wonderful to hold.

RUNE INTERPRETATIONS

Uruz: Strength
Power and vitality, endings and new beginnings. May indicate loss that is really disguised opportunity *Reversed* Lost opportunities or you are too easily led

Othila: Separation
Separation from anything to which overly attached. New direction *Reversed* Radical departure from old ways

Ansuz: The Messenger Rune
Awareness of what is to come, spiritual progress *Reversed* Problems with authority figures, lies, or deceptions

Gebo: Partnership
Indicates union of two wholes, and joy through sharing in its many aspects

Mannaz: The Self
From correct relationship with self, all other relationships flow *Reversed* Look inside to see why you are alone again

Algiz: Protection
Well-timed action and appropriate conduct protect. Help comes from unexpected quarter *Reversed* Vulnerability. Watch health and examine advice carefully

Eihwaz: Defense
A trying time. Signals a block, but in patient overcoming learn strength. In side-stepping, exercise wisdom

Inguz: Completion
Fertile time. Looks for resolution. Release from tension and old habit patterns

Nauthiz: Constraint
Assess limits you and others place on yourself. Need for restraint and rectification *Reversed* Revaluation of something disowned. Self-control is essential

Perth: Initiation
Deep transformative powers at work. On the material level, surprises may arise. At spiritual level, interior search matters *Reversed* Reveals guilty secrets

Teiwaz: Victory
The Spiritual Warrior. Taps into deepest resources bringing passion and adventure *Reversed* Danger through ill-timed or hasty action

Kano: Opening
Regeneration, brings light into dark places *Reversed* Freely give up something that has to pass away

Jera: Harvest
Beneficent, harvests what has been sown. Fruition comes slowly but surely. Certain knowledge that improvement follows

Wunjo: Joy
End of difficulties, positive outcome *Reversed* Delays

Fehu: Possessions
Prosperity and material gain. Rewards for past efforts and new opportunities *Reversed* What you have achieved may slip through your fingers

Raido: Communication
Indicator of travel, learning, and the soul's journey *Reversed* Signals caution and reassurance in personal relationships. Travel delays

Hagalaz: Chaos
Unexpected awakening through challenge. Disruption of plans

Laguz: Flow
Intuitive, instinctively knows what is needed. Follow flow to know yourself better *Reversed* Warns against over-reaching or giving in to temptation

Ehwaz: Progress
Transition, movement on all levels *Reversed* Timeliness is of the essence. Remember, there is an appropriate moment for everything

Berkana: Rebirth
New beginnings, renewal, and creativity *Reversed* Upheavals in the home. Are you putting your own needs above others?

Wyrd: Lap of the Gods
All possibilities are open. Life is what you make it – may indicate influences entirely outside your control

Sowelu: Wholeness
Power of the Life Force. Triumph over adversity; wholeness and self-realization. Counsels restraint and caution. Do not let ego take over

Isa: Standstill
Powerlessness and isolation. Time of waiting and surrender. Nothing else is possible

Dagaz: Breakthrough
Breakthrough, a transformation. Right outcome is assured. Major achievement and prosperity

Thurisaz: Gateway
Challenge, calls for patient nonaction *Reversed* Warns that careful consideration avoids wrong decisions or inappropriate action

Palmistry

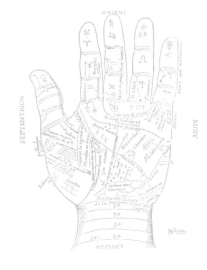

A palmistry diagram from Oeuvres by John Baptiste Pellow, printed in 1640.

The soul of man is in his hand.

COMPLETE BOOK OF THE OCCULT AND FORTUNE-TELLING

Palmistry, also known as chiromancy, is the art of reading fate in lines on the hand. It is believed that free will modifies that fate, which is why left- and right-hand lines may be different. The major lines correspond to vitality, temperament, and their consequences.

HANDLINES

A newborn baby has lines on the hands, formed in the womb at the same time as the facial features. These lines are believed to show the fate of that child. The lines may change as the child matures. In some systems of palmistry, one hand shows the fate one is born with, the other what is made of that fate. In people who lead an intense, intellectual life, the lines are stronger – although this can also be a sign of stress. The only people who do not have handlines are those who have been paralyzed. At death, the lines slowly disappear. The major lines are Life, Head, Heart, and Fate.

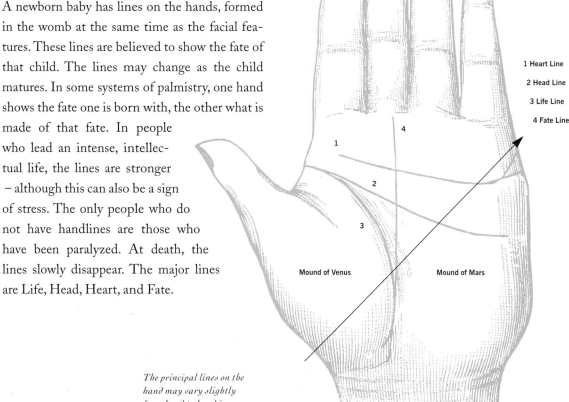

1 Heart Line

2 Head Line

3 Life Line

4 Fate Line

Mound of Venus

Mound of Mars

The principal lines on the hand may vary slightly from hand to hand in appearance and position, but are easily identified.

THE PRINCIPAL LINES

Palmistry was a popular and acceptable social art, as this eighteenth-century painting shows.

THE LIFE LINE

The Life Line starts above the thumb and curves around the Mound of Venus. This line indicates the vital energy a person has, together with possible length of life and serious accidents. However, although ages are assigned to different parts of the line, a short line should not be taken as an indication of an early death. A premature end to the line may indicate a complete change of life, and a break in the line a major life-changing event.

THE FATE LINE

The Fate Line starts above the wrist and goes up the center of the palm toward the middle finger. It means "that which happens comes" and relates to how a person manifests potential. It can indicate difficulties to be overcome. If the line indicates "hard times in old age" for instance, good pension provision would mitigate this. To find approximate ages, age thirty is where it crosses the Head Line and age forty to forty-five is where it crosses the Heart Line.

FATE LINE

Starts at wrist bracelets and rises straight up:
  Happy, calm life

Starts at Life Line: Happiness acquired by merit

Starts at Mound of Mars: Not easily discouraged

Strong line both hands: Success assured

Weak line: Person has to be self-reliant

Better at beginning than end: Hard times in old age

Irregular and many lines on hand:
  Extreme sensitivity creates difficulties

With many small lines alongside: Success,
  obstacles overcome

Made up of small lines: Indecision or illness

Broken, confused, cut: Changeable fate, capriciousness

Ascending branches: Life improves as one gets older

Stopping at Head Line: Rash acts or brain problems

Stopping at Heart Line: Affair of the heart affects position

If straight below middle
finger: Happy old age

If forked below middle
finger: Difficult old age

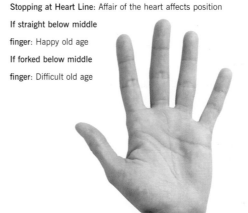

WHAT PALMISTRY CAN DO FOR YOU

The lines can tell you a great deal about your temperament and the possible course of your life, but it is emphasized that free will and making the best use of your potential can overcome even the most pessimistic of hand readings.

Astrology

Transits are used to pinpoint periods of change such as a major career move, a new house, a fresh relationship, or the unfolding of inner growth.

JUDY HALL: THE ILLUSTRATED GUIDE TO ASTROLOGY

Astrology has been used for prediction for eons and is based on close observation of repeating patterns and cycles. It is a way of knowing oneself and ascertaining possible events. Astrology goes back at least five thousand years, and the ancient astrologers were remarkably accurate in their predictions.

This twelfth-century book, Geometry of Astrology, *includes diagrams and descriptions of astrological measurements.*

AN ANCIENT SCIENCE

Western and Vedic (Indian) astrology have their roots in Babylon, Chaldea, and Egypt where astrology and astronomy were one single science. Chinese astrology, too, goes back at least four thousand years to the Emperor Yao. At first astrology was used for affairs of state, but gradually it expanded and was applied to individuals too. By the Middle Ages, the cosmic science was in use throughout the courts of Europe, the East, and China.

ASTROLOGY TODAY

Computer-generated birthcharts are easily obtained, some with standardized "year-ahead" interpretations. You can also consult an astrologer. Traditional Western astrology remains strong. In recent years there has been an upsurge of interest in Vedic astrology, rooted in "auspicious moments" from the ancient Vedas (religious texts). Although not much practiced in China nowadays, Chinese astrology has become popular in the West.

WHAT ASTROLOGY CAN DO FOR YOU

To truly benefit from astrology, you need a properly calculated horoscope. This will give you an in-depth picture of you, your strengths, weaknesses, potentials, and possibilities. You can also consult an astrologer as to the most beneficial place to live (Astro*Cartography), the most auspicious moment to start a new project or career, or for advice on financial and business trends.

Sun sign astrology in newspapers may be fun but is too general to be of individual benefit – except on rare occasions when the activities of the planets fit exactly into your personal chart. However, you can gain useful insights into energies operating in your life if you know where planets are on a day-to-day basis; and sun

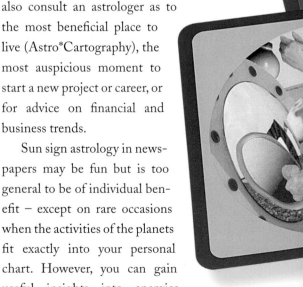

A natal chart showing signs, houses, planets, and aspects for a fateful moment in time: the start of a new millennium at Greenwich, London, England.

sign astrologers often refer to planets, indicating their effects on your sign. In addition, there are certain ages when everyone experiences a major "transit" (the effect of a planet in relation to the birthchart). If you know what to look out for at these ages, you can avoid the pitfalls and take advantage of favorable energies.

The majestic grandeur of Leo is shown visually in this example from the Zodiac Pack, together with the Descendant and Chiron, the wounded healer planet.

Western Astrology

In astrology, the signs of the zodiac express how celestial energies manifest through characteristics specific to each sign. The planets describe how easily that energy flows (for the purpose of astrology the sun and moon are called planets), and the "houses," which relate to the areas of life in which the effects of that energy will be visible. If the active and energetic planet Mars is passing through the fiery sign of Aries, for instance, it flows powerfully and strengthens the naturally impetuous Aries temperament. If Mars is transiting much quieter, dreamy Pisces its effect is considerably dampened down. With Mars in the first house, your personal life will become busier; if it is in the seventh house, you will meet passion or conflict in your relationships; and if it is in the tenth house these may manifest at work as your ambition is heightened.

DAY-TO-DAY PREDICTIONS

Western astrology uses several methods of ascertaining what may be in store for you. Most people are familiar with the horoscopes found in newspapers and magazines. These are based on the movement of the sun during the year and the effect of planets moving into and out of a sign and affecting, through a geometric relationship, other signs. However, there are more accurate means of pinpointing significant astrological events.

PROGRESSIONS

Progressions are symbolic movements of the planets at your moment of birth to allow for the time that has elapsed since birth. An astrologer will look at new relationships between planets, the movement of a planet into a different sign, and the interaction of the progressed chart with the natal chart to ascertain changes.

TRANSITS

The day-to-day movements of the planets overhead are called transits. Although transits do not actually cause things to happen, it feels as if they do! The effect of a planet transiting a planet or house in your chart is to set in motion the energies of that planet or that house. So, if transiting Mars is roaring past your natal Sun or Uranus, you may well become accident prone. If Saturn is aspecting your Moon, you may find

Sun	Self-expression, fulfillment, life force, manifestation	**Saturn**	Responsibilities, duties, burdens, lessons, ambitions
Moon	Feelings, intuition, instincts, cycles, home, parents	**Uranus**	Sudden change, stress, insight, transformation
Mercury	Thoughts, speech, communication, business matters	**Neptune**	Ideals, dreams, illusions, deceptions, the arts
Venus	Love life, beauty, creativity, social life, women	**Pluto**	Elimination, death, birth, sex, regeneration
Mars	Action, dynamic energy, men, accidents, willpower	**South Node**	The karmic past, ingrained habits
Jupiter	Luck, good fortune, expansion, opportunity, excess	**North Node**	The karmic future, soul purpose

yourself prey to deep, dark depression. When Jupiter passes through your tenth house, you may experience sudden promotion or find a much better job.

Each chart is individual, so day-to-day transits need to be interpreted from your own unique chart. However, there are certain ages when the planets return to their natal place, or are opposite in the zodiac, setting off predictable life changes.

THE JUPITER RETURN

This happy event occurs every twelve years (age 12, 24, 36, etc.). It is the beginning of a new cycle of opportunity. Things are put in motion on a Jupiter Return. For the next three years you work at it. Then you are able to see if it has flourished. If it has, you harvest the rewards for six to nine years. After nine years, the cycle begins to close to make way for a new opportunity.

A similar cycle operates between transiting Jupiter and your natal Sun (the place where your Sun was at your birth). This cycle starts at whatever age Jupiter first reaches your Sun, and then occurs regularly every twelve years thereafter.

THE SATURN RETURN

The first Saturn Return occurs at the age of twenty-eight or twenty-nine. Saturn is a strict disciplinarian and this is a time of personal reassessment and commitment. You ask: "Where have I got to in life? Am I on my path? Am I doing what I should be?" If not, you may find yourself retraining. It is also a time when many people take on more responsibility whether at work or at home.

The Second Saturn Return occurs at age fifty-seven or fifty-eight, a time when many people are preparing for retirement and "old age." As "old age" may last another thirty years or so, the same questions apply and new answers have to be found.

The Third Saturn Return coincides with another major event, the Uranus Return.

SIGNS

Aries
Energetic, confident, ebullient, egocentric, passionate

Taurus
Reliable, loyal, practical, productive, secure, stubborn

Gemini
Adaptable, quick, light-hearted, sociable, dual, talkative

Cancer
Sensitive, protective, moody, sympathetic, nurturing

Leo
Dramatic, open, regal, proud, generous, playful

Virgo
Analytical, modest, discriminating, efficient, critical

Libra
Diplomatic, harmonious, cooperative, partnership-led

Scorpio
Intense, deep, magnetic, powerful, secretive, sexual

Sagittarius
Optimistic, questioning, adventurous, humorous, tactless

Capricorn
Careful, ambitious, controlled, responsible, disciplined

Aquarius
Unconventional, independent, idealistic, humanitarian

Pisces
Fluid, emotional, intangible, vacillating, malleable, imaginative

ASTROLOGICAL HOUSES

1
Personal life and appearance

2
Finances and values

3
Siblings, neighbors, communication, short journeys

4
Home and family

5
Leisure time, children, affairs

6
Health, vocation, daily routines

7
Partners and relationships of all kinds

8
Shared resources, inheritances, death

9
Travel, beliefs, philosophy, long journeys

10
Career, aims, social status, environment

11
Friends, social activities

12
Unconscious thoughts, secrets, institutions

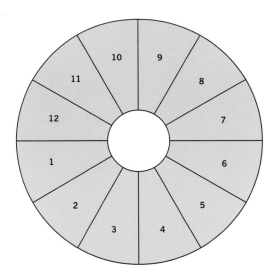

The houses relate to the areas of life listed left.
The houses are read anticlockwise starting from 1.

THE URANUS OPPOSITION

Because Uranus is a highly unpredictable planet, this occurs anywhere between age thirty-eight and the middle forties depending when you were born and where Uranus is in its eliptical orbit. This is often a time of major stress and change, abrupt endings and new beginnings, yet it offers great possibilities of transformation. The urge is to let go of all that is outworn and outgrown from the past. Those who resist or avoid what they know to be true and important can find themselves suffering heightened stress and even illness. However, if you cooperate with your insights, you move into something new.

THE URANUS RETURN

This momentous event occurs at age eighty-four. If you have left undone something you should have done, this is the time when it suddenly becomes apparent. If you are doing something you should no longer be doing, it ceases – abruptly. Life sweeps you into drastic changes just when you thought you were getting past all that!

ASTROLOGY IN THE PALM OF YOUR HAND

Astro-Dice combine the wisdom of astrology with the excitement of rolling dice. There are three twelve-sided dice, one for the planets, one for the zodiac signs, and one for the astrological houses. The planet represents what is happening; the sign, how it feels; and the house, the area of life that is being affected.

WHAT ASTRO-DICE CAN DO FOR YOU

In addition to giving you surprisingly clear guidance as to what is happening, or about to happen, in your life, Astro-Dice can also help you to learn astrology without really trying. What they cannot do is give yes-or-no answers.

USING ASTRO-DICE

Using Astro-Dice could not be simpler. You throw the three dice, keeping your question in mind if you have one. You use the symbol that is uppermost. Read the "planet" first (use the Planets chart to help you). The Astro-Dice pack includes interpretations, but an astrology book, such as *The Zodiac Pack*, will give further amplification. The planet indicates the energy available to you. The "sign" (read this second) represents how the planetary energy will manifest; and the "house" (read this last) shows which area of your life is affected. Bring the three together and you have the basis of your answer.

VISUAL ASTROLOGY:
THE ZODIAC PACK

The Zodiac Pack is an astrology pack, not Tarot cards. It is a unique, visual approach to learning, and understanding, astrology intuitively. It brings astrology graphically to life. The images on the cards tell you what the planets, signs, and houses are all about. You don't need to know anything about astrology to use the pack, which provides incredibly deep insight into who you are and where your future is leading.

With the Zodiac Pack you lay out your birthchart visually, in pictures. You can put in on the floor, walk around in it, explore different parts of it, meditate with it, and attune to all the different parts of yourself. You can use it to integrate inherent contradictions and to find hidden potential. You can pick cards up and walk them around to their new, progressed position. Or, with an extra set of planetary cards, you can feel the effect of a passing planet moving through one of the houses of your chart or activating a birth-planet. No words are needed, but the book accompanying the pack is an in-depth astrology course with all the information you need to totally understand astrology, your birthchart, yourself, and other people.

The Zodiac Pack enables you to lay out your chart in pictures, graphically showing you who you are and where your future lies. It is also the basis of meditations to attune to the meanings of signs, planets, and houses.

WHAT THE ZODIAC
PACK CAN DO FOR YOU

The Zodiac Pack takes you straight into the center of yourself. It brings immediate insights into who you are, and what you are capable of. It deepens both your understanding of astrology and your intuition. It is particularly helpful when you are trying to understand your relationship with someone else and can revolutionize your relationships with family, lovers, colleagues, and friends.

Chinese Astrology

Chinese astrology is based on a twelve-year zodiac, with specific characteristics and fortunes, and a longer, sixty-year cycle that influences your life according to where you were born within the cycle. Correspondences and oracles are also utilized for divination and guidance. You can easily identify the animal sign under which you were born and your auspicious direction and time of year.

Year of the Rat

1936 Jan 24 to Feb 10 1937
1948 Feb 10 to Jan 28 1949
1960 Jan 28 to Feb 14 1961
1972 Feb 15 to Feb 2 1973
1984 Feb 2 to Feb 19 1985
1996 Feb 19 to Feb 6 1997
2008 Feb 7 to Jan 25 2009

Personality: Lively, intelligent, and quick to spot opportunities. Gregarious, open, and humorous, nevertheless guards privacy. Excellent organizer. Needs to be appreciated, craves security. Can be critical. **Career:** Versatile and clever, enjoys sales, accountancy, publishing, outdoor pursuits. Handles small projects better than large-scale ones. **Direction:** North. **Season:** Winter.

Year of the Pig

1935 Feb 4 to Jan 23 1936
1947 Jan 22 to Feb 9 1948
1959 Feb 8 to Jan 27 1960
1971 Jan 27 to Feb 14 1972
1983 Feb 13 to Feb 1 1984
1995 Jan 31 to Feb 18 1996
2007 Feb 18 to Feb 6 2008

Personality: Honest, affectionate, and supportive. Looks for best in people. Initially reserved but wide circle of friends. Tolerant, avoids arguments, can stand ground. **Career:** Studious, unambitious. Hardworking and cooperative, avoids strife and risks. Caregiver. Enjoys law, medicine, research, social work, gardening. **Direction:** North-north-west. **Season:** Early winter.

Year of the Dog

1934 Feb 14 to Feb 3 1935
1946 Feb 2 to Jan 21 1947
1958 Feb 18 to Feb 7 1959
1970 Feb 6 to Jan 26 1971
1982 Jan 25 to Feb 12 1983
1994 Feb 10 to Jan 30 1995
2006 Jan 29 to Feb 17 2007

Personality: Empathetic, sensitive, honest, and courageous. Dislikes injustice. May be over-critical but offers good advice. Strong sense of duty. Overwhelmed by things beyond own control. **Career:** Conscientious and trustworthy. Dislikes competitive situations. Good team member and can take lead. Suited to law, social work, education, counseling, medicine, and campaigning. **Direction:** West-north-west. **Season:** End of autumn/fall.

Year of the Rooster

1933 Jan 26 to Feb 13 1934
1945 Feb 13 to Feb 1 1946
1957 Jan 31 to Feb 17 1958
1969 Feb 17 to Feb 5 1970
1981 Feb 5 to Jan 24 1982
1993 Jan 23 to Feb 9 1994
2005 Feb 9 to Jan 28 2006

Personality: Charming, well-groomed, likes attention. Compassionate and independent. Strong opinions, hates advice. May be erratic and vulnerable beneath confident front. Tendency to overspend. **Career:** Logical, dislikes pressure, and needs time to think. Ideal own boss. Enjoys public relations, sales, politics, entertainment. **Direction:** West. **Season:** Mid-autumn.

Year of the Ox

1937 Feb 11 to Jan 30 1938
1949 Jan 29 to Feb 16 1950
1961 Feb 15 to Feb 4 1962
1973 Feb 3 to Jan 22 1974
1985 Feb 20 to Feb 8 1986
1997 Feb 7 to Jan 27 1998
2009 Jan 26 to Feb 13 2010

Personality: Quiet, steady, and tenacious. Practical and stubborn, often in a rut. Cautious, honest, sincere. Takes on others' problems. **Career:** Dislikes competition, does not seek financial gain. Pays attention to detail. Skilled and logical, likes routine. Enjoys gardening, farming, religion, teaching, medicine. **Direction:** North-north-east. **Season:** End of winter.

Year of the Monkey

1932 Feb 6 to Jan 25 1933
1944 Jan 25 to Feb 12 1945
1956 Feb 12 to Jan 30 1957
1968 Jan 30 to Feb 16 1969
1980 Feb 16 to Feb 4 1981
1992 Feb 4 to Jan 22 1993
2004 Jan 22 to Feb 8 2005

Personality: Lively, intelligent, aware. Good company, enjoys variety. Trustworthy but wily, opportunistic. **Career:** Adaptable and versatile, quick reactions. Creative and well-organized. Good at assessing financial risk and rising to challenges. Enjoys investigation, media, public relations, management, finance. **Direction:** West-south-west. **Season:** Early autumn.

Year of the Tiger

1938 Jan 31 to Feb 18 1939
1950 Feb 17 to Feb 5 1951
1962 Feb 5 to Jan 24 1963
1974 Jan 23 to Feb 10 1975
1986 Feb 9 to Jan 28 1987
1998 Jan 28 to Feb 15 1999
2010 Feb 14 to Feb 2 2011

Personality: Positive, optimistic, and enthusiastic. Enjoys challenges and unexpected events. May misjudge or misplace trust. Can become critical or suspicious. **Career:** Determined and enthusiastic, enjoys initiating projects. Good leader, does not deal well with failure. Suited to travel, politics, design, or business. **Direction:** East-north-east. **Season:** Beginning of spring.

Year of the Ram

1931 Feb 17 to Feb 5 1932
1943 Feb 5 to Jan 24 1944
1955 Jan 24 to Feb 11 1956
1967 Feb 9 to Jan 29 1968
1979 Jan 28 to Feb 15 1980
1991 Feb 15 to Feb 3 1992
2003 Feb 1 to Jan 21 2004

Personality: Gentle and trustworthy, equable but sensitive. Avoids unnecessary conflict. Happy wanderer, unconventional. Takes pleasure from simple things. **Career:** Has ability to turn fortunes around. Dislikes routine work, rigid schedules. Artistic and creative. Suits arts, research, advertising, publishing. **Direction:** South-south-west. **Season:** End of summer.

Year of the Rabbit

1939 Feb 19 to Feb 7 1940
1951 Feb 6 to Jan 26 1952
1963 Jan 25 to Feb 12 1964
1975 Feb 11 to Feb 30 1976
1987 Jan 29 to Feb 16 1988
1999 Feb 16 to Feb 4 2000
2011 Feb 3 to Jan 22 2012

Personality: Tranquil and sensitive, dislikes competition or aggression. Anxious if forced to take risks. Retiring but hospitable, charming host. Generous nature turns enemies into friends. **Career:** Conscientious worker. Dislikes "cut and thrust" and pressure, suited to calm creativity. Enjoys art, design, public relations, literature, counseling, law. **Direction:** East. **Season:** Mid-spring.

Year of the Dragon

1940 Feb 8 to Jan 26 1941
1952 Jan 27 to Feb 13 1953
1964 Feb 13 to Feb 1 1965
1976 Jan 31 to Feb 17 1977
1988 Feb 17 to Feb 5 1989
2000 Feb 5 to Jan 23 2001
2012 Jan 23 to Feb 9 2013

Personality: Charismatic, enthusiastic, lively, and self-confident. Proud. Outspoken and decisive. Enjoys being center of attention. Highly successful, blessed with good fortune. **Career:** Likes responsibility, excellent leader. Needs challenge and freedom. Good entrepreneur. Enjoys management, law, and arts. **Direction:** East-south-east. **Season:** End of spring.

Year of the Snake

1941 Jan 27 to Feb 14 1942
1953 Feb 14 to Feb 2 1954
1965 Feb 2 to Jan 20 1966
1977 Feb 18 to Feb 6 1978
1989 Feb 6 to Jan 25 1990
2001 Jan 24 to Feb 11 2002
2013 Feb 10 to Jan 30 2014

Personality: Active and decisive. Stimulated by intelligent debate, bored by superficial chatter. Excellent judge of situations. Dislikes being proved wrong. Quick to anger. **Career:** Hardworking but enjoys breaks. Alert to new possibilities, works independently, negotiates well. Enjoys law, politics, catering, psychology. **Direction:** South-south-east. **Season:** Early summer.

Year of the Horse

1930 Jan 30 to Feb 16 1931
1942 Feb 15 to Feb 4 1943
1954 Feb 3 to Jan 23 1955
1966 Jan 21 to Feb 8 1967
1978 Feb 7 to Jan 27 1979
1990 Jan 27 to Feb 14 1991
2002 Feb 12 to Jan 31 2003

Personality: Independent, gregarious, and impulsive. Eloquent speaker, inspired by ideas. Impulsive, easily flattered. Indiscreet. Confident façade can hide inner doubts. **Career:** Good team player. Initiates projects but does not always follow through. Suited to mentally or physically demanding work. Enjoys sport, sales, and construction. **Direction:** South. **Season:** Mid-summer.

Numerology

The idea of vibration, described by number, is central to numerology.

PAUL RODRIGO

Numerology uses numbers to analyze personality and predict events. The vibration of your birth number determines your temperament. Each number carries a particular vibration, odd numbers are more powerful and therefore regarded as masculine, even numbers are softer and feminine.

THE ORIGINS OF NUMEROLOGY

Modern numerology has its origins in sixth-century BCE Greece. The philosopher and mathematician Pythagoras, founder of geometry, asserted that number was the essence of all things. He attributed specific personalities to numbers, as well as unique vibrations. Pythagoras also believed in the immortality of the human soul and its reincarnation from life to life. He divided souls into nine characteristic types, the numbers of which are still used today.

FINDING YOUR NUMBER

To determine your number, add together the digits of your birth date. The first step is to write the date in number form. The century has to be written in full, not abbreviated. So, if you were born on **1 November 1985**, you would write down: **01.11.1985** – or, U.S. style, **11.01.1985.** The next step is to write it out as the sum of all digits: **1+1+1+1+9+8+5.** Add them together: **26.**

Add these digits together: **2 + 6 = 8.** The birth number is **8.** Each number has both positive and negative traits associated with it.

YOUR NAME NUMBER

You can also work with a number obtained from your name. To start with, total the number from your full name at birth. Use the table to find the number for each letter of your full birth name. Then add these numbers together until you are left with a single digit (as for your birth number).

Next total the number for the name you are known by now and see what the difference is. Many people select a new name for themselves, or add initial letters only to their name, so that they obtain a favorable number for their present stage of life.

1	2	3	4	5	6	7	8	9
A	B	C	D	E	F	G	H	I
J	K	L	M	N	O	P	Q	R
S	T	U	V	W	X	Y	Z	

NUMBER CYCLES

A numerological reading will also involve the cycle of life you are in, as each nine-year cycle affects you in specific ways. The new cycle begins on your birthday. To find which year of the cycle you are in, write your birthday and month and, instead of the year of your birth, put the present year. Add them together. This is the cycle year you are now in. You can substitute any year and look back to see which cycle you were in when specific events occurred, or forward to see what the future might hold. So, 1 November birthdays would add **1 + 1 + 1 + 2 + 0 + 0 + 1 = 6** to see which year 2001 was. Looking at the cycle, it is a year of vision and acceptance.

THE NINE-YEAR CYCLE

1 Creativity and Confidence

2 Cooperation and Balance

3 Expression and Sensitivity

4 Stability and Process

5 Freedom and Discipline

6 Vision and Acceptance

7 Trust and Openness

8 Abundance and Power

9 Integrity and Wisdom

PERSONALITY NUMBERS

1 Self-confident showperson. Independent, single-minded, natural ability, successful, high standards, passionate, fulfilled
Negative: Egocentric, opinionated, frustrated tyrant, lonely, bitter

2 Compassionate, selfless, loving, faithful, warm-hearted, carer, discreet, sound judgment, peace loving, unambitious
Negative: Over-sensitive, secretive, self-doubting, vindictive, stubborn, hypochondriac

3 Cheerful, optimistic, generous, charming, vivacious, versatile, quick thinker, romantic, dutiful
Negative: Superficial, naïve, easily exploited, hypocritical, over-indulgent, fickle

4 Virtuous, dutiful, conventional, loyal, ambitious, efficient, resourceful, practical, romantic, prudent
Negative: Rigid, sanctimonious, thoughtless, greedy, ruthless, manipulative, disillusioned

5 Elusive, volatile, adaptable, curious, convivial, adventurous, independent, amorous, creative
Negative: Vague, wayward, erratic, unemotional, irresolute, verbose, wasted talent

6 Charismatic, realistic, fair-minded, urbane, contented, idealistic, resourceful, seductive
Negative: Ostentatious, manipulative, self-indulgent, complacent, lethargic, inhibited

7 Private, introspective, witty, wise, analytical, generous, honest, prudent, careerist
Negative: Withdrawn, isolated, dogmatic, calculating, blunt, unimaginative

8 Self-reliant, intense, reserved, practical, honest, fair, powerful, destined
Negative: Isolated, misunderstood, outspoken, obsessional, stubborn, envious, insecure, controlling

9 Vital, enthusiastic, bold, emotional, innovative, reflective, ambitious, lustful, energetic
Negative: Rash, impulsive, insecure, accident prone, quarrelsome, disingenuous, slapdash, rebellious, autocratic

Native American Medicine

The indigenous people of North America . . . have a great deal to teach us,
since they have kept their connection with Mother Earth and all her creatures,
and with the Creator, Great Spirit.

ELIANA HARVEY

The Native American people incorporated oracles into their way of life. It was part of "Medicine," an all-embracing web woven of all life together. Medicine increased spiritual connection, connected each part with every other part of the whole, and brought about healing and harmony.

MEDICINE

While the various tribes had slightly different teachings, an underlying belief in Medicine united the indigenous peoples of North America. Medicine is anything that improves one's connection to the Great Mystery and all life. It includes healing mind, body, and spirit. It is anything that brings personal power and an understanding of how to use it. It is the living of life in perfect harmony with the Whole.

THE MEDICINE WHEEL

The Medicine Wheel represents the unity of all life. It is a sacred enclosure and is divided into four areas, the "directions," North, South, East, and West. Specific powers, qualities, and energies reside in different parts of the wheel and spiral around it. A Medicine Wheel is a map, it gives internal direction. It is not only North, South, East, and West but also "places in-between," a linking point for different worlds.

A ceremonial medicine wheel carefully laid out in the stunning — and sacred — landscape of Sedona, Arizona.

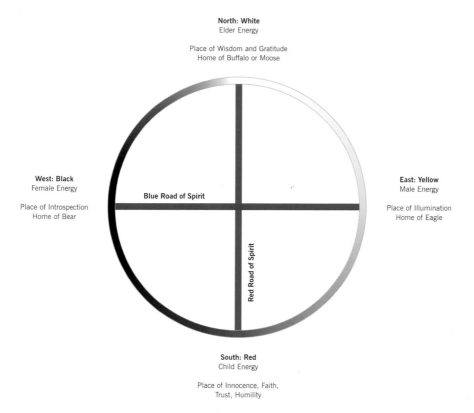

North: White
Elder Energy

Place of Wisdom and Gratitude
Home of Buffalo or Moose

West: Black
Female Energy

Place of Introspection
Home of Bear

Blue Road of Spirit

Red Road of Spirit

East: Yellow
Male Energy

Place of Illumination
Home of Eagle

South: Red
Child Energy

Place of Innocence, Faith,
Trust, Humility

THE MEDICINE WALK

The Medicine Walk is a way of reestablishing links with Medicine Helpers and deepening intuition. Traditionally the walk was taken through the forest observing signs and portents along the way. Today it is guided by cards representing those same omens.

WHAT NATIVE AMERICAN MEDICINE CAN DO FOR YOU

Native American Medicine is a profound system of being. It can be taken out of context and used purely as an oracle – if you see an animal you can look up its meaning, for instance, or you can draw a card for guidance. But to get the most benefit from the Medicine packs, you need to understand the background against which the cards are set. All the packs help you to do this. As Jamie Sams (creator of The Medicine Cards and The Sacred Path Cards) says: "It involves walking on the

Earth Mother in perfect harmony with the Universe." Using Medicine brings healing, harmony, support, a recognition of the wholeness of life, and sensitivity to the needs of the environment.

A Blackfoot woman from Idaho USA in traditional dress.

The Medicine Cards

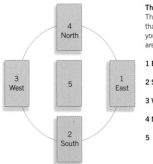

36 Lizard
Dreaming
Reversed
Inner conflict

The Native North Americans honor every living being as a teacher. The Medicine Cards call on that teaching through animals. In their habits lie messages and knowledge of life lessons. These life lessons are pathways to power.

PATHWAYS TO POWER

Power allies are teachers. The more you can connect with an animal, the greater the knowledge it can pass to you. You can learn to call on the medicine it brings to empower you, and to access specific talents.

USING THE MEDICINE CARDS

There are layouts to help you connect to your animal allies and totem animals, to understand where your life is going, to bring balance into your life, and to predict the outcome of projects. The book accompanying the pack has subtle and insightful interpretations. After a moment's quiet reflection and centering, the cards are shuffled and spread out face down on the table. Cards are drawn according to intuition and placed in an appropriate spread. When you interpret the cards, remember that reversed cards indicate an imbalance.

Nine Totem Animals
The nine totem animals represent the medicine you carry on your earth walk, showing qualities your spirit seeks to express. In addition to the seven cards, there are two other animals. These will be represented by cards to which you are especially drawn, or by animals not in the pack but with whom you resonate. There are blank cards in the pack so that you can add your own animal(s).

1 East	Greatest spiritual challenge. Path to illumination
2 South	Protection for the child within. Trust
3 West	Personal truth. Path to goals
4 North	Wise counsel
5 Above	Access to other dimensions
6 Below	How to stay grounded and on path
7 Within	How to find your heart's joy
Left	Protector of the female side. Courage and warrior energy
Right	Protector of the male side. Relationships and mothering

Butterfly Spread
This layout helps you to ascertain the outcome of projects.

1	Past
2	Present
3	Future
4	Pattern or lesson moving through
5	Challenge or lesson completed
6	What is working for you
7	What is working against you

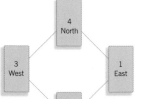

The Medicine Wheel Spread
The Medicine Wheel reveals things that you need to reflect upon in your personality and in what you are learning.

1 East	Spiritual strength and direction. Major challenge
2 South	What you need to trust in yourself
3 West	Internal solution to challenge
4 North	How to spiritually apply and integrate lessons
5	Where you are standing

Pathway Spread
This spread gives you overall information about your life.

1 East	Seed of the idea. Is it needed now?
2 South	What needs to be done. Will the energies be great enough to overcome obstacles?
3 West	Higher purpose. What is it serving?
4 North	The place of manifestation. What is to be gained?

1 Eagle
Spirit
Reversed Seek
lofty ideals

 10 Turtle
Mother Earth
Reversed Reconnect

 19 Buffalo
Prayer and
Abundance
Reversed Seek
help to receive

 28 Armadillo
Boundaries
Reversed Allow
vulnerability

 37 Antelope
Action
Reversed Listen
to the Spirit

 2 Hawk
Messenger
Reversed Open Up

 11 Moose
Self-esteem
Reversed Know the
wisdom of silence

 20 Mouse
Scrutiny
Reversed Attend
to details

 29 Badger
Aggressiveness
Reversed
Inappropriate anger

 38 Frog
Cleansing
Reversed Take
a break

 3 Elk
Stamina
Reversed Beware
overstretching

 12 Porcupine
Innocence
Reversed Loosen up

 21 Owl
Deception
Reversed
What are you
in the dark about?

 30 Rabbit
Fear
Reversed
Release fears.

 39 Swan
Grace
Reversed
Pay attention
to your body

 4 Deer
Gentleness
Reversed Learn
to love

 13 Coyote
Trickster
Reversed Beware

 22 Beaver
Builder
Reversed Open doors

 31 Turkey
Give away
Reversed Cultivate
generosity

 40 Dolphin
Manna
Reversed Remember
to breathe

 5 Bear
Introspection
Reversed Reclaim
inner knowing

 14 Dog
Loyalty
Reversed Become
your own best friend

 23 Opossum
Diversion
Reversed Caught
in a drama

 32 Ant
Patience
Reversed
Beware conmen

 41 Whale
Record keeper
Reversed Reconnect
to your knowing

 6 Snake
Transmutation
Reversed Blocking
change

 15 Wolf
Teacher
Reversed Expand
limited view

 24 Crow
Law
Reversed Lying
to yourself

33 Weasel
Stealth
Reversed
Beware intrigue

42 Bat
Rebirth
Reversed
Stagnation

 7 Skunk
Reputation
Reversed Avoid
arrogance

16 Raven
Magic
Reversed Seek
healing

25 Fox
Camouflage
Reversed Beware
apathy

34 Grouse
Sacred Spiral
Reversed Dissipation
of energy

43 Spider
Weaving
Reversed
Honor your mate

8 Otter
Woman Medicine
Reversed Unfocused
female energy

17 Mountain Lion
Leadership
Reversed Playing
with fire

26 Squirrel
Gathering
Reversed A hoarder

   **44 Hummingbird**
Joy
Reversed
Closed heart

35 Horse
Power *Reversed*
Reclaim power
through compassion

 9 Butterfly
Transformation
Reversed Recognize
change

 18 Lynx
Secrets
Reversed Watch
your tongue

 27 Dragonfly
Illusion
Reversed Caught
in illusion

Sacred Path

*Guardian of an
ancient path, a lone
bison stands beneath
wide open skies ready
to aid a vision quest
or council fire.*

*Sacred Path Cards offer a deepening of the teachings in the Medicine Cards.
They are a guide to making the Medicine Walk. The cards present questions to develop your own
intuitive guidance. They point to lessons learned along the way, and to the teachers you meet
during your spiritual development.*

5
Personal freedom to be gained

4
Mental attitude

EARTH CONNECTIONS

The originator of the Sacred Path Cards intended them to bring about harmony and love between the whole of creation. She feels that the environment can be healed by reconnecting to the Earth, allowing different nations to understand each other better.

USING SACRED PATH CARDS

Sacred Path Cards are designed to recreate a Medicine Walk, a pathway of initiation. They can be used outdoors in a natural setting, or indoors supplemented by imagination.

Each of the cards you meet brings you new insight. They are the omens and teachers you would meet on an actual Medicine Walk. You can combine them with the Medicine Cards for even deeper insights.

There are no reversed cards because each card is intended to help you come to your own personal truth. The cards are held upright and shuffled side to side, then placed face down in a fan. Approaching the cards quietly and intuitively helps you to select the appropriate cards. Layouts can be taken from the Medicine Cards or from the book accompanying

8
Successful completion,
abilities gained

7
Unexpected challenge

6
Needs met and
prayers answered

5
Medicine needed

4
Structure required

3
Future

2
Tipi front door.
Present

1
Past

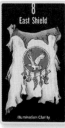

Tipi Spread

the Sacred Path Cards. Each of the Sacred Path layouts gives you a different viewpoint on your path. The cards can also be used as a "daily lesson," drawing one card for the day.

PEACE TREE SPREAD

The Peace Tree Spread is used when you are feeling at odds with your environment or yourself. It shows what is needed for inner peace. Card 1 uncovers a talent you are not acknowledging, which creates confusion and unease.

3
Physical lessons

Peace Tree Spread

2
Strength to be gained

1
Buried Talent

TIPI SPREAD (LEFT)

The Tipi Spread gives an overall view of your life lessons and reveals the future impact of those lessons. It clarifies your position in the world.

Card 2 represents the present lesson, Card 5 the medicine you can call on, Card 7 the unexpected challenge in the situation, and Card 8 what you will gain.

1	**Pipe**
	Prayer, inner peace. Balancing the self
2	**Sweat Lodge**
	Purification. Gentle cleansing
3	**Vision Quest**
	Seeking, finding. New directions
4	**Peyote Ceremony**
	New abilities. Enhance growth
5	**Standing People**
	Roots, giving. Connect to Mother Earth
6	**Sun Dance**
	Self-sacrifice. Restore sacredness
7	**Medicine Wheel**
	Cycles, movement. Where you are
8	**East Shield**
	Illumination, clarity. Find order
9	**South Shield**
	Innocence, inner child. Lighten up
10	**West Shield**
	Introspection, goals. Know your own answers
11	**North Shield**
	Wisdom, gratitude. New understanding
12	**Arrow**
	Truth as protection. Stay on path
13	**Coral**
	Nurturing. Reconnect to feelings
14	**Kokopelli**
	Fertility. Create
15	**Talking Stick**
	Viewpoints, options. Open up
16	**Power Place**
	Earth connection, empowerment. Catalyzer
17	**Moon Lodge**
	Retreat. Take a break
18	**Whirling Rainbow**
	Unity, wholeness achieved. Remove discord
19	**Painted Face**
	Self-expression. Emerge
20	**Counting Coup**
	Victory. Challenge overcome
21	**Rites of Passage**
	Change. Recreate
22	**Heyokah**
	Humor, opposites. Trickster energy

23	**Smoke Signals**
	Intent. Walk your talk
24	**Council Fire**
	Decisions. Do it now
25	**Powwow**
	Sharing, quickening. Gather the like-minded
26	**Warbonnet**
	Advance. Move forward
27	**Cradleboard**
	Ability to respond. Find your own answers
28	**Medicine Bundle**
	Allies, support. Honor ancestors
29	**Story-teller**
	Expansion. Be your potential
30	**Fire Medicine**
	Passion, spontaneity. Acknowledge fire within.
31	**Medicine Bowl**
	Healing. Good medicine
32	**Drum**
	Rhythm, internal timing. Realign
33	**Dreamtime**
	Unlimited vision. Take flight
34	**Burden Basket**
	Self-reliance. Become self-reliant
35	**Shawl**
	Returning home. Remember self
36	**Thunder-beings**
	Usable energy. Energized
37	**Great Mystery**
	Original source. Cocreatio.
38	**Field of Plenty**
	Ideas, needs manifested. Abundance
39	**Stone People**
	Records, knowing revealed. Memories bring awareness
40	**Great Smoking Mirror**
	Reflections. Leave the myth behind
41	**Shaman's Death**
	Death and rebirth. Let go
42	**Hour of Power**
	Ritual of joy. Celebrate life
43	**Give-away Ceremony**
	Release. Share what you have
44	**Sacred Space**
	Respect. Happiness begins within

White Eagle MedicineWheel

The White Eagle Medicine Wheel is a journey of spiritual awakening taken in the company of Wa-Na-Nee-Che, a Lakota Medicine teacher. It operates on three levels of learning and attainment: Apprentice, student, and elder.

A PATH OF BEAUTY

In the traditional Lakota way, understanding the Medicine Wheel would come about through simple, practical daily tasks performed alongside sacred rituals. It also incorporated teaching stories, such as the Creation of Mother Earth. Wa-Na-Nee-Che says that in this way pupils learn to walk a path of beauty, a path on which it is not what is achieved that matters, but how it is achieved.

THREE LEVELS

At the apprentice level, the teachers are twenty-eight animals, of which one might become your power animal. You are learning how to bring balance and harmony into your life.

The Elders, seven Grandfathers and seven Grandmothers, teach at student level. Here you develop your own abilities and personal qualities, deepening and widening your spiritual growth. At elder level, four archetypal symbols or totems teach. You learn to take full responsibility for your life, making clear choices rather than being at the mercy of others.

HOW TO USE THE WHITE EAGLE MEDICINE WHEEL

The cards represent the teachers and carry their spirit energy. To attune to them, various spreads and visualizations are used as you work through

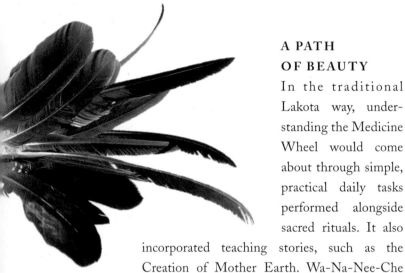

Bear
Power, wisdom, dreams, and visions

Snake
Rebirth, creative force, sexuality

Butterfly
Sensitivity, positiveness, transformation

Gateway Spread

Helper

Vision

Skills needed

Factors holding you back

Animal card · EAGLE ·

Grandmother card · STARGAZER ·

Grandmother card · SPIRIT WARRIOR ·

Guide for Journey

Reversed Animal card · BUFFALO ·

Gateway Spread
Gateway helps you find new opportunities or beginnings

Grandfather card · WEAVER ·

the different levels guided by the words of Wa-Na-Nee-Che. The White Eagle Medicine Wheel provides a living teaching of self-discovery, ceremony, and visions. It is designed to be used as an ongoing inspirational tool rather than an oracle that is used only once but it does also aid problem-solving and healing.

Cards are selected from their appropriate levels rather than being shuffled all together. When reversed, the cards show obstacles along the way.

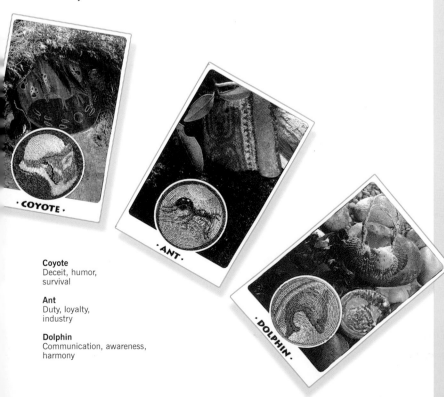

Coyote
Deceit, humor, survival

Ant
Duty, loyalty, industry

Dolphin
Communication, awareness, harmony

THE CARDS

Eagle
Vision, fearlessness, expansion

Bear
Power, wisdom, dreams, and visions

Badger
Tenacity, anger, healing

Beaver
Industry, flexibility, creativity

Spider
Patience, balance, weaving of energy

Horse
Power, energy, freedom of spirit

Buffalo
Protection, stubbornness, generosity

Otter
Playfulness, trust, feminine intuition

Rabbit
Timidity, anxiety, alertness

Porcupine
Gentleness, trust, innocence

Cougar
Strength, assertiveness, leadership

Dragonfly
Mystery, illusion, self-deception

Dog
Intelligence, loyalty, friendship

Turtle
Realism, stability, protection

Elk
Self-esteem, strength, bringer of dreams

Whale
Gentleness, intelligence, intuitive knowledge

Fox
Speed, cunning, awareness

Moose
Authority, maleness, unpredictability

Raven
Mysticism, magic, clairvoyance

Hummingbird
Joy, music, love

Owl
Wisdom, insight, discernment

Hawk
Perception, foresight, information

Grandfather Pipe Carrier
Spiritual retreat

Grandfather Dreamweaver
Dreaming visions

Grandfather Sundancer
Compassion and endurance

Grandfather Medicine Man
Healing vibrations

Grandfather Spirit Warrior
Protection

Grandfather Provider
Gratitude and respect

Grandfather Record Keeper
Seek truth

Grandmother Weaver
Richness of life

Grandmother Birther
Creative flow

Grandmother Medicine Woman
Connection with Mother Earth

Grandmother Stargazer
Wider picture

Grandmother Wisdom Keeper
Inner knowing

Grandmother Rainbow Dancer
Personal rhythm

Grandmother Story-teller
Wisdom of the ancient ones

Sweat Lodge
Cleansing, healing, renewal

Drum
Energy, rhythm, movement

Medicine Wheel
Seeing, understanding, energy

Totem Pole
Lineage, mythology, spirituality

The Mayan Oracle

The Mayan symbols are part of the galactic coding and seeding for the creation of the light body.

ARIEL SPILSBURY AND MICHAEL BRYNER

At the height of their power, the Mayans built vast cities and pyramidal temples, reflecting intricate cosmology, and employing mathematical and astronomical knowledge, the subtleties of which are still being discovered. They developed a complex calendar covering a span of twenty-six thousand years, encoded along with the remnants of other texts on the walls of their temples, and huge, carved stelae (standing stones).

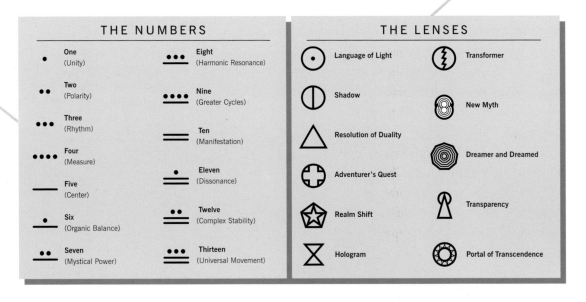

THE NUMBERS		THE LENSES	
One (Unity)	**Eight** (Harmonic Resonance)	Language of Light	Transformer
Two (Polarity)	**Nine** (Greater Cycles)	Shadow	New Myth
Three (Rhythm)	**Ten** (Manifestation)	Resolution of Duality	Dreamer and Dreamed
Four (Measure)	**Eleven** (Dissonance)	Adventurer's Quest	Transparency
Five (Center)	**Twelve** (Complex Stability)	Realm Shift	
Six (Organic Balance)	**Thirteen** (Universal Movement)	Hologram	Portal of Transcendence
Seven (Mystical Power)			

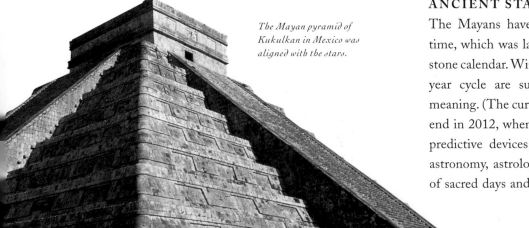

The Mayan pyramid of Kukulkan in Mexico was aligned with the stars.

ANCIENT STAR IMAGES

The Mayans have a cyclical understanding of time, which was laid down in their great sacred stone calendar. Within the twenty-six-thousand-year cycle are subcycles, each of which has meaning. (The current great cycle is calculated to end in 2012, when a new cycle will begin.) The predictive devices the ancient Mayans used – astronomy, astrology, numerology, the counting of sacred days and cycles of the calendar – were indivisible. Their symbols served as a key to understanding the universe.

In remote Guatemalan highlands, this system is still used. "Daykeeper priests" work with the sacred calendar, twenty-day, or "star" glyphs, and thirteen numbers. They cast small crystals and stones, experiencing a physical sensation called "blood lightning" as confirmation. The Mayan Oracle is a visionary interpretation of ancient Mayan symbols.

USING THE MAYAN ORACLE

The oracle comprises twenty archetypal star glyphs, thirteen numbers, and eleven "lenses," which offer new ways of looking at oneself and the world. One or more cards are drawn and the energies are worked with through meditation or the readings and exercises within the manual. It is an essential part of using the oracle that the energies of the symbol be attuned to and integrated within yourself.

Each card has three "resonances," or levels, at which it can be read. Magic Child is poetic and intuitive. Discoverer is more oracular and speaks directly to the concerns of daily life; and Journeyer takes you much deeper into the energies of the symbols.

WHAT THE MAYAN ORACLE CAN DO FOR YOU

The Mayan Oracle incorporates Ascension, the idea that humanity is developing a light body to enter a new spiritual dimension beyond that known up to now. It is not an idea or a system that suits everyone but if you resonate with this belief and the symbols speak to you, then it is claimed that the oracle will help you with a physical and consciousness transformation that will take you into a new dimension of being.

IMIX
Source of life, divine nurturance and support, primordial Mother, undivided primal waters, primal trust and nourishment, receptivity

IK
Spirit, breath, wind, inspiration, presence, truth, coordinator of reality, simplicity, unseen forces, integration of polarities

AKBAL
Abyss, mystery, sanctuary, serenity, "looks within," place enclosing darkness, journey into self, stillness, Dreamtime, dreamfield matrix, dream exploration

KAN
Seed, seedling manifestation, self-germination, creation, fertile ground, gestation, opening, erupting possibility

CHICCHAN
Vitality, passion, sensing, body wisdom, motivation, desire, instinct, creativity, serpent power, kundalini, integration, purification, intimacy

CIMI
Surrender, release, death, transmutation, forgiveness, humility, revelation

MANIK
Completion, gateway, opening, beauty, identification, dance, mudra, divination, acting "as if," spiritual tools, priest/priestess

LAMAT
Harmony, starseed, beneficial combinations, way shower, octave, expanded love, clear perspective

MULUC
Signals, signs, awakened attention, awareness, understanding, self-remembrance, divine guidance, Godseed, cosmic communication, beacon

OC
Breakthrough, new beginnings, relationships, companions of destiny, emotional-body issues, recasting the past, spiritual strength, guardians and guides

CHUEN
Innocence, spontaneity, inner child, humor, artistry, monkey, trickster, disruption, transparency

EB
Abundance, harvest, chalice, emptiness, open vessel, quickening

BEN
Fluid reference points, time/space traveler, skywalker, angelic messenger, pillars of heaven, courage, new directions, mysterious journey

IX
Integrity, heart-knowing, alignment with divine will, magician, shaman, jaguar, night seer, priest, torch bearer, magic

MEN
Hope, commitment, compassionate service, global consciousness, dreams and visions, planetary mind, belief in oneself

CIB
Grace, trust, inner voice, galactic conduit, reception, mystic transmission, divine communication, cosmic consciousness, golden pillar, ferryman's staff

CABAN
Centeredness, synergy, synchronicity, Earth force, galactic alignment, Earth keeper, fluid world resonance, clue tracking, crystal healing, shield

ETZNAB
Timelessness, discrimination, clarity, hall of mirrors, spiritual warriorship, sword of truth, facing shadow, integration of paradox

CAUAC
Purification, transformation, reunion, light body, activation for ascension, thunderbeing, lightning path, initiation by fire, ecstasy of freedom

AHAU
Union, wholeness, ascension, unconditional love, solar mastery, Christ consciousness, language of light ecstasy, limitless bliss, crown

The Mayan Oracle

Ancient British Auguries

Methods of divination were widely used by the Celtic peoples; auguries of animals and their movements, the shapes of clouds, forms of lot-casting, scrying in the elements, the wisdom of trees, and the prophecies of poets were all used to help guide decisions or to ascertain the will of the gods.

CAITLIN MATTHEWS: CELTIC WISDOM

The Celts were an ancient people who inhabited the British Isles long before the Romans arrived. Their central tenet was a belief in the immortality of the soul. This is a belief that may well have come from the people who lived in the isles long before the Celts arrived and who built stone circles that reveal a sophisticated knowledge of astronomy.

This example of the Green Man was carved in the east cloister of Norwich Cathedral in 1415 by John Watlington with Brice the Dutchman but the origins are much older.

ANCIENT BRITONS

The ancient Briton's understanding of the world is one of the oldest systems of all. Early in their history, the British Isles were invaded by wave after wave of conquering peoples. This pushed the "old religion" back to the wildest, most remote regions, but traces of it linger in the Green Man carved on fonts and church doorways, in May Day rituals, and in the decking of homes with evergreens at Yuletide.

When the Celts arrived in the Bronze Age, the Druidic religion was flourishing. The Druids were soothsayers and workers of magic. Their arcane symbols and deep understanding of archetypes were incorporated into Celtic oral tradition – the Celts did not use writing as such, although the Druids had their own alphabets, as did other ancient British people.

The Celts themselves came from central Europe, bringing their own traditional knowledge with them, a system that had its most

King Arthur, the legendary English king, who ruled in the sixth century CE.

*Sir Galahad on his quest for the Holy Grail,
painted in 1870 by Arthur Hughes.*

ancient roots in India. When Christianity first arrived in the islands, the ancient Celtic wisdom was incorporated into Celtic Christianity. Celtic saints were dowsers, healers, and workers of miracles, appropriate successors to the Druids.

THE ARTHURIAN LEGACY

Throughout the Middle Ages, Celtic wisdom was incorporated into the Arthurian legends, along with Romano-British motifs. The Grail Knights spoke about universal matters and performed an archetypal quest: A spiritual search that still calls seekers today.

WHAT ANCIENT BRITISH ORACLES CAN DO FOR YOU

The pre-Celtic, Celtic, and Arthurian divination systems are spiritual and nature-based. Powerful auguries in their own right, the packs that have brought this knowledge to the fore once more help you to attune to the cycle of the year and the eternal spiritual quest, and to find your deepest roots. They offer a practical system for working magic: A change in consciousness.

The Celtic Tree Oracle

The cards that comprise the Celtic Tree Oracle are based on the ancient British Ogham alphabet. The twenty-five letters of this alphabet, also known as Beth-Luis-Nuin, have the names of trees or other natural objects. The Ogham alphabet has now been translated into an augury for the modern world.

DRUIDIC DIVINATION

This system of divination was created by the Druidic priests around 600 BCE and remained in use until the fourteenth century CE. The letters were cut into wood or carved on

One of a group of monoliths inscribed with Ogham characters – named after Ogma, a god associated with the magic power of the word – found near Coláiste Ide, Co. Kerry, Ireland.

stones, some of which still survive. The alphabet could also be used as a sacred sign language for secret communications.

The Ogham alphabet is symbolic of Celtic cosmology and the cycle of life. The names of the thirteen Ogham letters correspond with the names of the thirteen months of the Celtic lunar year, which began in November with the month of Beith (Birch). The Ogham Beith represents a new start.

MAGICAL ROOTS

To the Druids the Ogham alphabet was more than an alphabet, it was a symbolic code, a key to open a door into a parallel world of knowledge, meanings, and associations. Ogham tapped into the subconscious or group mind.

USING THE ORACLE

Traditionally this oracle would be used at the time of the new moon or on one of the eight Celtic festivals. It was never used on a daily basis or to ask too many questions. If you wished to view the year ahead, the appropriate time would be Samhain (November 1). Because the method of working and the interpretation are complex, the book accompanying the pack is required to gain full benefit from the oracle.

B
Beith (Birch)
Month: November
A new start, cleansing

M
Muin (Vine)
Month: August
Prophecy

CH
Koad (Grove)
A sacred place, all knowledge available, past present, and future

L
Luis (Rowan)
Month: December
Protects against enchantment, controls senses

G
Gort (Ivy)
Month: September
Spiral of the self, search for self

TH
Oir (Spindle)
Sweetness and delight, sudden intelligence

F
Fearn (Alder)
Month: January
Oracular and protective

NG
NGetal (Reed)
Month: October
Direct action

PE
Uilleand (Honeysuckle)
Hidden secret

S
Saille (Willow)
Month: February
Night vision, lunar rhythms, female aspects

Ss
Straif (Blackthorn)
No choice, cleansing

PH
Phagos (Beech)
Old knowledge, old writing

N
Nuin (Ash)
Month: March
Inner and outer worlds linked

R
Ruis (Elder)
Month: Last 3 days of October
The end in the beginning and the beginning in the end

XI
Mor (The Sea)
The sea, travel, maternal links

H
Huathe (Hawthorn)
Month: April
Cleansing, chastity, protection

A
Ailim (Silver Fir)
High views and long sight

D
Duir (Oak)
Month: May
Solid protection, doorway to mysteries, strength

O
Ohn (Furze)
Good at collecting, a magpie

T
Tinne (Holly)
Month: June
Best in the fight

U
Ur (Heather)
Links to inner self, all heal

C
Coll (Hazel)
Month: July
Intuition, straight to the source

E
Eadha (White Poplar)
Helps rebirth, prevents illness

Q
Quert (Apple)
Choice of beauty

I
Ioho (Yew)
Rebirth, eternity

The Greenwood Tarot

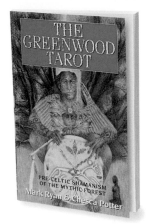

The Greenwood Tarot is a beautifully crafted pack by the illustrator of The Celtic Shaman's Pack. Its symbols are powerful and archetypal, based on long experience in working ancient magic. They go back to pre-Celtic days.

The imagery used in the Greenwood Tarot goes back to the pre-Celtic era.

The Wheel of the Year reflects the natural turning of the seasons.

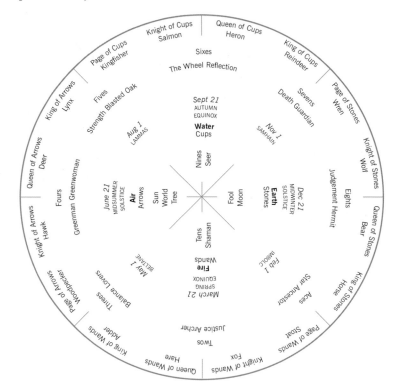

THE WHEEL OF THE YEAR

The natural turning of the seasons, movement and migration of animals, physical effects of elements, and the environment had a deep effect on the ancient Britons. The rhythm of the year was harnessed for festivals, magic, and religious working – and has been revived in a Tarot pack that is rich in shamanic wisdom and alive with forest lore.

The Greenwood Tarot is set in Greenwood Forest and follows the Wheel, introducing the archetypal figures who inhabit it. Three areas act as different levels of consciousness and gateways. The Inner Wheel is inhabited by *The Fool*, *The Shaman* and *The Seer*, and *The World Tree*. Above is *The Sun* of midsummer, below is *The Moon* of midwinter. On the Wheel itself, two archetypes rest at each quarter and cross quarter points, on an inner/earth and an outer/universal consciousness level. Attuning to each level takes you on your own journey round the year.

THE GREENWOOD JOURNEY

The journey is guided by *The Fool*. It starts at Imbolc on February 1, new beginnings after long winter. The first

The Fool

archetype is *The Ancestor*, a guardian and a guide to the tangled forest landscape. On the outer level, *The Star* fixed in the sky reminds travelers to hold their true direction.

At Spring Equinox, March 21, *The Archer*, symbol of new life, emerges with boundless energy. Here you learn about willpower and how

The Lovers

to focus your desires and aims. On the outer level, *Justice* reminds you of the responsibility involved in your actions. At Beltane, May 1, *The Lovers* unite two energies to create a third. On the outer

Balance

level *Balance* (intertwining and yet independent forces), bring change and equilibrium.

At Midsummer Solstice, June 21, the resplendent and all-powerful *Greenman* and *Greenwoman* emerge, representing the human species at the height of its power, and the abun-

Greenman

Greenwoman

dance of nature. By Lammas, August 1, it is time for harvest. The energy naturally starts to withdraw. Preparation and maturity lie within *The Blasted Oak*. It is time to burn off old bonds and cleanse the soul. *Strength* is gained through endurance, the resilience of nature itself.

Strength

By Autumn Equinox, September 21, you reach inner *Reflection* and *Healing*. Feelings of anger or frustration are relinquished and trust develops. Fate makes itself known through *The Wheel*. At Samhain, November 1, it is time to deal with the darker elements of your nature, to honor and prepare for *Death*. *The Guardian* greets you with his dark riddles and sardonic humor. He represents the wildness of your own nature and strips away comforting perceptions of yourself.

When Midwinter Solstice, December 21,

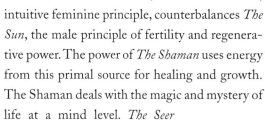

The Moon

approaches, you embrace *The Hermit* and withdraw to healing silence in the forest to find inner wisdom. *Judgment* awaits, and you reap what you have sown.

The Moon, with its reflective,

The Sun

intuitive feminine principle, counterbalances *The Sun*, the male principle of fertility and regenerative power. The power of *The Shaman* uses energy from this primal source for healing and growth. The Shaman deals with the magic and mystery of life at a mind level. *The Seer*

The Shaman

The Seer

comes from the visceral world of emotion and intuition. She swims beneath the surface of the unknown. When the two integrate, the gateway opens to *The World Tree*. The tree is entered through its roots, connecting to the inner universal mind and the outer reaches of the cosmic mysteries. This reunites the sacred inner divinity and ignites your own personal connection to universal creation. (The pack also includes other characters and spreads to aid your journey.)

The World Tree

Celtic Wisdom

These three packs come from the wisdom of John and Caitlin Matthews, experts in Celtic tradition and Arthurian lore. Each pack approaches Celtic wisdom from a slightly different direction but all offer a profound understanding of the archetypal forces at work in ancient British consciousness and their relevance to today.

CELTIC WISDOM TAROT

Derived from authentic source texts, this powerful pack helps you to explore the prophetic mysteries of the Bard, Druid, and Seer. The visual format upholds the ancient oral tradition. It depicts the soul's transformational journey as it spirals through initiations by Celtic gods and Ogham trees in the Wisdom Cards (the Major Arcana). These cards show the deep archetypes, aspects, and thresholds of the Celtic Otherworld.

The Story Cards (the Minor Arcana) tell of Celtic heroes and heroines, and the adventures of bardic legend, revealing the more mundane life and the rich variety of human experience. The cards are divided into Battle, Skill, Art, and Knowledge – the four major activities of Celtic people. When the Wisdom and Story packs are shuffled together, they bring about a mingling of deep spiritual change and daily circumstance, revealing the circuit of the soul. In Celtic tradition, the soul came forth from the cauldron of rebirth complete with its own innate qualities and gifts – and these are symbolized by the cards.

THE CELTIC SHAMAN'S PACK

This pack helps you to enter a magical realm where everything is sacred. This realm holds the answers to deep and challenging questions unfolded by the shaman's visionary path, developing your own latent shamanic skills along the way.

THE CROW

The practice of shamanism involves working closely with the natural world and The Celtic Shaman's Pack provides gateways to elemental and spirit worlds.

XIX THE PROTECTOR

The Protector in Celtic Wisdom (left) asks who you are in your true self, while The Crow from the Celtic Shaman (above) represents change and is the appropriate totem animal to accompany you when making new decisions.

One of the lesser powers, Sword Hallow stands for incisive energy and cutting through illusions while King Arthur stands for wielding power in the greater world.

All shamans spend much of their time walking paths between three worlds: The physical, elemental, and the spiritual. The pack maps out this territory. All you need to enter and explore the space between the worlds is the belief that you are a spiritual being living in a spiritual universe.

Shamans carry shamanic tools such as bones, stones, or ritual items, and The Celtic Shaman's Pack provides the tools you need for your journey and guides its process. The forty cards are divided into suits of Movers – representing you and the tasks you have taken on; Empowerers – beings who support you in your journey into the inner realms; Worlds – three levels within which the shaman moves; Elements – the kingdoms of earth, air, fire, and water; Totem Beasts – the shaman's helpers; and Shapers – recurring archetypal patterns. One additional card, The Card of Vision, links the three worlds and directs your journey.

THE ARTHURIAN TAROT

Steeped in the unrivaled magic of the legends, history, and traditions of Arthurian Britain, these wonderfully evocative cards capture the wonder and beauty of King Arthur's realm and reveal the Arthurian mysteries as a living mythos for creative visualization, soul growth, and personal transformation through The Hallowquest.

The images on the Major Arcana, Greater Powers, come from Celto-Arthurian legend and the characters that peopled the court. These cards are the inner voices of dreams and guardian angels. They do not speak of mundane matters, but rather represent archetypal or Otherworldly concerns. When cards from the Major Arcana appear in a spread, they urgently draw attention to the fact that you are part of the greater creation and ask you to take a good look at the overall patterns that your life is making.

The Minor Arcana, Lesser Powers, are based on the landscape of Britain itself and, while the suits, or Hallows, show the quest for spiritual wholeness, these cards speak plainly and mundanely. They show general direction and the ways in which you make your path easier or more difficult. Swords, Spears, Grails, and Stones are the empowering objects of the inner quest.

Original spreads based on a Celtic understanding of the world enable you to make your own quest and explore your life.

Ancient Egyptian Oracles

The achievements of the Egyptians are indicative of an extraordinary leap of
consciousness that humankind has passed through, and this period of history may even give
us clues to the greater process of human evolution.

DAVID LAWSON: EYE OF HORUS

Egyptian religion was a magical practice, full of omens and portents. In everyday life, too, the gods were seen to be at work. Indeed, the gods and goddesses were part of everyday life. There was no separation between the spiritual and the physical. The deities represented archetypal forces that manifested through all things.

THE MAGICAL LIFE

The ancient Egyptian religion was a magical one. Rituals were practiced, spells recited, and oracles consulted. Words, spoken or written, had power. Offerings were made, and bargains were struck between human and god. For Egyptians, magic was a potent force. Omens were given great import. What today might be dismissed as mere superstition was, for them, a way of communicating with the gods.

Temple practice invoked the power of the deity. The priests spoke to the gods on behalf of the people, and interpreted the reply. If someone was ill, a priest was consulted. If he declared that it was the work of the gods, nothing could be done. If it was not, then the power of the gods would be invoked to aid sophisticated healing methods. The gods would predict a favorable outcome – or not.

POTENT FORCES

The gods were not known merely as remote deities. They were archetypal forces that manifested in everything and everyone. Their energy could be harnessed, and modern Egyptian oracles use this power for divination and self-understanding. The hieroglyphs are imbued with magical force. In using the oracles, you have the opportunity to tune in to the great power of those ancient gods – and this can be life-changing.

Tutankhamun's burial chamber, showing offerings being made to Osiris, Lord of the Dead, and magical hieroglyphic instructions for navigating the next world.

The Eye of Horus hovers over the Pharaoh's ka, the part of his soul that would make the journey into another world.

WHAT EGYPTIAN ORACLES CAN DO FOR YOU

Egyptian oracles help you to understand how you shape your own future. They point to adjustments that can be made to improve that future, and show you unconscious forces and beliefs that might be acting against your best interests. One oracle, The Eye of Horus, gives you affirmations to change your mental attitude and stimulate your spiritual growth. Cartouche cards can be used as an oracle or as a talisman to draw specific energies into your life. Both oracles require meditations for attunement.

The Eye of Horus

The Eye of Horus contains twenty-five stone tablets designed to be used as an oracle of personal vision, personal development, creativity, and spiritual growth.

ARCHETYPAL PICTURES

Twenty-three of the tablets depict the gods and goddesses of ancient Egypt in symbolic form, based on their hieroglyphs. Their essence is timeless and universal. The two remaining tablets show the pyramids and the sphinx, images with a powerful impact today. The twenty-five tablets make sense of your own personal journey, reflecting the world around you and your inner development. They may also represent the attributes of a person coming into your life. Each has affirmations, the myth, symbolism, attributes, and an attunement meditation.

USING THE EYE OF HORUS

The tablets are mixed in the bag provided. Close your eyes and breathe deeply, asking for the stones to bring illumination and wisdom. Specific questions can be focused on. A stone should be selected without looking at it. Place it in front of you. Notice whether it is upright or reversed. Reverse readings are concerned with the effect that you have upon others, how you are viewed, and your current influence within the world at large.

A single tablet can view the day ahead, the week, or the month. You can also pick a stone for a specific project or to represent a person. There are five layouts with the pack, each designed to meet a different need.

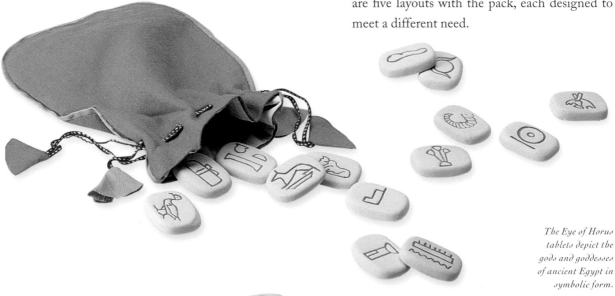

The Eye of Horus tablets depict the gods and goddesses of ancient Egypt in symbolic form.

The Eye of Horus Spread is used only once, since it is a personal totem of power, creativity, and spiritual purpose. It clarifies fundamental questions such as "Why am I here?," and the original reading can be returned to many times for further clarification. The other spreads look at relationships, challenging decisions, and future trends.

Yourself in relationship

The other in the relationship

1 Basic personality, drives, motivation

2 Face that has been assumed

3 The most powerful life lesson

4 Blueprint for spiritual development

5 Personal power, special gifts

6 Greatest challenges

7 Ultimate spiritual direction

Relationship Spread

THE TABLETS

Geb	*Properties*	Ecology, nourishment, parental judgment.
	Attributes	Authority, trust, reliability
Nut	*Properties*	Mystery, firmament, sustenance, laughter
	Attributes	Fun, friendly, full of ideas, enthusiastic
Osiris	*Properties*	Might, universal power, fertility, continuing life
	Attributes	Stability, personal power, confidence
Isis	*Properties*	Devotion, magical skills, motherhood, loyalty
	Attributes	Maternal, devoted, loyal
Seth	*Properties*	Rebellion, destruction, rivalry, sovereignty
	Attributes	Foreign, alien, different
Nephthys	*Properties*	Shadow, guardianship, retreat, grief
	Attributes	Power, dedication, silent exterior, sweet nature
Horus	*Properties*	Vision, majesty, communication, balance
	Attributes	Visionary, fun, inspirational, humorous
Bastet	*Properties*	Perfume, purity, peacefulness, affection
	Attributes	Affectionate, caring, aloof, self-contained, compelling
Anubis	*Properties*	Healing, guidance, lightness of spirit, protection
	Attributes	Compassionate, good-humored, reassuring, fun
Hathor	*Properties*	Destiny, love, birthright, music
	Attributes	Fun-loving, frivolous, caring
Amun	*Properties*	Invisibility, supremacy, manifestation, strength
	Attributes	Powerful impact, enigmatic, mysterious
Re	*Properties*	Journeying, cycles, illumination, creation
	Attributes	Charismatic, attractive, purposeful
Khonsu	*Properties*	Wandering, youthfulness, pathways, provision
	Attributes	Eternally youthful, attractive, innocent
Khnum	*Properties*	New life, language, creativity, procreation
	Attributes	Artist, craftsperson, creative
Hapy	*Properties*	Fullness, abundance, fluidity, ebb and flow
	Attributes	Caring, supportive, sensitive
Maat	*Properties*	Truth, justice, morality, integrity
	Attributes	Fair, impartial, well balanced
Khepri	*Properties*	Emergence, motivation, propulsion, adornment
	Attributes	Self-contained, purposeful, strong
Anat	*Properties*	Courage, fearlessness, vigor, sexuality
	Attributes	Forceful presence, stranger
Min	*Properties*	Sexuality, fruitfulness, renewal, regeneration
	Attributes	Seductive, fun, flirtatious
Heket	*Properties*	Birth, midwifery, quickening, the home
	Attributes	Gentle, practical, protective
Apis	*Properties*	Power, proclamation, messages, protection
	Attributes	Amiable, easygoing, accepting
Meretseger	*Properties*	Mercy, honesty, respect, seclusion
	Attributes	Forgiving, tolerant, with clear boundaries
Imhotep	*Properties*	Administration, instruction, skill, deification
	Attributes	Organizer, diplomat, technical/creative genius
The Pyramids	*Properties*	Group consciousness, geometry, symbolism, wonder
	Attributes	Shared spiritual origins and destiny
The Sphinx	*Properties*	Secrets, enigma, longevity, patience.
	Attributes	Long-lived, continually present, confident

Cartouche

Cartouche is a French word describing the oblong "box" in which the names of Pharaohs are inscribed. The twenty-five Cartouche cards encapsulate the archetypal ideas of the Egyptians in ways that are easily recognizable in modern times. They act as a bridge between the everyday self and the higher self.

6 Spiritual future

4 Most important
life so far

*Using the Star for
Past Life Information*

THE CARDS

The first nine cards of Cartouche represent the major archetypes. These are forces that govern the universe as well as psychological principles. Cards 11 to 25 represent more mundane energies. Card number 10 represents Set, the negative force. It can represent your own opposition to something new or unforeseen problems.

The cards can be interpreted at the spiritual or superconscious level; the psychological, mental, or subconscious level, and the material, mundane, or conscious level. Reversed cards can indicate that the energies they represent are being negated or inverted. They act as a warning.

2 Basic soul
nature

5 Soul's progre
to date

USING CARTOUCHE

The cards can be used for meditation, divination, healing, dream interpretation, and accessing past lives. They are shuffled, cut, and laid out in spreads including the horoscope wheel and the versatile Star Spread.

3 Role chosen by the soul

TALISMANS

What is different about Cartouche is that single cards can be used as a talisman. The Egyptians had some very effective ways of protecting their property. All the cards have a talismanic function and some are especially potent: *Bast* protects the mind during divination; *Hathor's Mirror* reflects negative energies back to their source; *Nephthys* makes you "invisible" so that you can walk in safety and, placed above the door, it discourages unwanted visitors to your home. *Anubis* protects home and person. Carry it if you have to walk alone through dark or lonely places. Left in your hallway, it protects your house.

1 Osiris
Upright   Wisdom, justice, integrity, stability, responsibility
Reversed   Unreliability, religious mania, delusions of grandeur

2 Isis
Upright   The magical arts, compassion, caring, maternal perseverance
Reversed   Superstition, lack of concern, love, overpossessiveness, insularity

3 Horus
Upright   Physical healing, courage, heroism, harmony, artistry, beauty, creativity, family
Reversed   Vengeance, timidity, eccentricity, discord, insecurity, narcissism

4 Bast
Upright   Intuition, caution, protection, devotion, mental healing, generosity, gracefulness, joy
Reversed   Insensitivity, remoteness, recklessness, sadness, lack of coordination

5 Thoth
Upright   Fate, karma, healing, health, law, scholarship, education
Reversed   Misfortune, ill-health, conceit, quackery, pseudo-intellectual

6 Hathor
Upright   Fortitude, nourishment, femininity, astrology, organization, confidence
Reversed   Vacillation, intimidation, deprivation, vanity

7 Nephthys
Upright   Mysticism, receptivity, psychic gifts, tranquillity, reservedness
Reversed   Diffusion, psychosis, tension, deviousness, illusion

8 Ptah
Upright   Ingenuity, masculinity, craftsmanship, inventiveness, dexterity
Reversed   Banality, chauvinism, destructiveness, misogyny

9 Anubis
Upright   Diplomacy, navigation, humor, protection
Reversed   Vulnerability, tactlessness, misguidance, foolhardiness

10 Set
Upright   Opposition, delay, problems
Reversed   Malign intent

11 Fire
Upright   Energy, creativity, loyalty, valor, ardor
Reversed   Inertia, sterility, disloyalty, quick temper

12 Air
Upright   Intellect, travel, communication, speed, commerce
Reversed   Ignorance, detachment, lack of concentration

13 Water
Upright   Emotions, fluidity, sympathy, reflection
Reversed   Immaturity, stagnation, callousness, easily led

14 Earth
Upright   Industry, thrift, conservation, money, possessions, practicality, growing things
Reversed   Idleness, parsimony, waste, dourness, miserliness

15 Sirius
Upright   Universal awareness, pioneering, adventure, stamina, physical strength
Reversed   Bigotry, stubbornness, aggressiveness, lack of stamina

16 Lotus
Upright   Continuity, meditation, placidity
Reversed   Fragmentation, introversion, agitation

17 Crook and Flail
Upright   Self-discipline, authority, worldly status
Reversed   Hedonism, domination, bossiness

18 Uraeus
Upright   Occult adept, sagacity, honesty
Reversed   Occult fakery, deceitfulness, cunning, folly.

19 Winged Disk
Upright   Divine guidance, inspiration, achievement
Reversed   Self-deception, blind obedience, failure.

20 The Twins
Upright   Polarity, integration, partnership, marriage
Reversed   Egocentricity, divisiveness, separation

21 Sphinx
Upright   Secrecy, observation, patience
Reversed   Indiscretion, inattentiveness, cruelty

22 Scarab
Upright   Renewal, adaptability, acceptance
Reversed   Neglect, rebellion, resentment

23 Pyramid
Upright   Initiation, timelessness, preservation
Reversed   Regression, limitation, corruption

24 Ankh
Upright   Life Force, understanding, emotional love
Reversed   Infatuation, rejection, withdrawal, death

25 Buckle of Isis
Upright   Fidelity, fertility, growth with sacrifice
Reversed   Inconstancy, selfishness, barrenness

Aboriginal Dreaming

·19 Wombat·

> The animals, plants, and creatures of our land are our ancestors, our brothers and sisters, mothers and fathers. We call them our totems.
>
> PAULINE E. MCLEOD, STORY-TELLER

·40 Seal·

One of the oldest living cultures uses symbols and signs for an oracle.

The images in Aboriginal Dreaming come from an ancient wisdom tradition. Turtle is a symbol of a safe retreat in times of difficulty and the ingenuity to get yourself out of trouble.

THE ORACLE OF THE DREAMTIME

The Aboriginal people believed the world was full of signs from Spirit. To them the world was a living oracle. If a creature crossed their path, it brought a message. If clouds formed a pattern, it had meaning. These oracles were connected to the Dreamtime, or Dreaming. The Dreaming is a spiritual energy underlying all things. And at the same time, everything has its own unique energy field. Because there was no written language, the visual signs and symbols of the oracles were passed on in artwork and story form. These ancient stories have now been incorporated into an Oracle of the Dreamtime so that they are accessible to modern users. The cards are illustrated by Aboriginal artists and incorporate both traditional and modern symbolism with a profound depth of meaning.

USING THE ORACLE

The oracle consists of circular cards that have an upright or reversed meaning. They can be shuffled and the creator of the oracle recommends cutting them into three piles. The first pile represents the past, the second the present, and the third the future. How many cards are in each pile helps you to judge how much the past is influencing the

·5 Rainbow Serpent·

present or if there is a lot of meaning invested in the future. The "future pile" is then placed on the "past" and the "present pile" placed on top. Cards are dealt into various layouts. The book accompanying the pack gives detailed layouts and very subtle interpretations.

WHAT ABORIGINAL DREAMING CAN DO FOR YOU

The symbols and cards are a tool for self-exploration. They explore ways of solving problems and challenge you to look honestly at the reality you are creating. The cards can be used for meditation and dream interpretation, and to form a visual symbol of an energy you seek. The oracle includes the appropriate Australian Bush Flower Essence for each card, and these essences can be used to bring about profound healing.

The circular cards of the Oracle of the Dreamtime, illustrated by Aboriginal artists, incorporate both traditional and modern symbolism.

1 Gymea Lily
Responsibility,
sacrifice, hope

2 Lightning Man
Warning, impacts,
power

3 Moon
Cycles, changes,
gestation

4 Opal
Justice, spiritual law,
karma

5 Rainbow Serpent
Creation, transformation,
spirituality

6 Seven Sisters
Initiation, tests,
conviction

7 Southern Cross
Death, endings,
spiritual belief

8 Sturt's Desert Pea
Intuition, tragedy,
loss

9 Sun
Perpetual motion, journeys,
awakening

10 Uluru
Power, center,
balance

11 Waratah
Grief, devotion,
love

12 Dingo
Independence, lessons,
emotions

13 Echidna
Sharing, selfishness,
irritations

14 Emu
Competition, status,
self-esteem

15 Frill-neck Lizard
Personal power,
ego, magic

16 Kangaroo
Kindness, consideration,
gentleness

17 Koala
Secrets, restraint,
respect

18 Spider
Illusions, seduction,
charisma

19 Wombat
Home, security,
boundaries

20 Bat
Chauvinism,
fixed viewpoints, anger

21 Black Swan
Victimization, assistance,
miracles

22 Bogong Moth
Curiosity, journeys,
advice

23 Brolga
Creativity, dance,
expression

24 Brush Turkey
Resentment, comparisons,
introspection

25 Butterfly
Transformation, spirituality,
emergence

26 Crow
Trickery, distractions,
the mind

27 Gray Owl
Protection, honor,
special talents

28 Kookaburra
Reliability, work,
satisfaction

29 Lyrebird
Imitation, learning,
pride

30 Magpies
Inspiration,
solutions, light

31 Rainbow Lorikeet
Overcoming disability,
limitations, release

32 Sea Eagle
Manifestation,
focus, will

33 Willy Wagtail
Communication,
messages, gossip

34 Barramundi
Love, union,
wholeness

35 Crab
Self-transformation,
preparation, shapeshifting

36 Crocodile
Respect,
heartlessness

37 Dolphin
Unconditional love,
freedom, mockery

38 Frog
Humor,
laughter, play

39 Platypus
Diplomacy,
tolerance, unity

40 Seal
Environment, resources,
exploitation

41 Turtle
Retreat, safety,
ingenuity

42 Whale and Starfish
Strategy, betrayal,
selfishness

43 Ocher
Magnetism, courage,
artistic expression

44 Reconciliation
Harmony, equality,
acceptance

45 Sydney Harbor Bridge
Structure, technology,
achievement

Scrying

Each crystal is unique, carrying its own particular theme and frequency

STEPHANIE HARRISON AND BARBARA KLEINER: CRYSTAL WISDOM

Scrying, which means "revealing," uses crystals, mirrors, flames, or water to look into the future. Early humans were buried with crystal mirrors which, it was believed, could see into another realm. Crystals balls, too, have been found in ancient graves. Bowls of water and candles have been a divination aid for hundreds of years.

The image of a dark woman staring into the crystal ball has its roots in prehistory when the tribal seer peered into a crystal or pool to discern the future.

THE CRYSTAL GAZER

The Crystal Gazer presents an enduring image. A dark, gypsy-like woman gazing into a crystal ball and asking to have her palm crossed with silver. She has her roots way back in prehistory when the seer of the tribe peered into a crystal or pool. In ancient Britain, Tibet, Babylon, Egypt, and elsewhere, seers would gaze into the mirror-like surface of water. In South America, the Aztec God of Magic, Tezcatlipoca has a name that means "mirror that smokes" – an allusion to the mist that forms in the crystal.

NOSTRADAMUS

The sixteenth-century astrologer and seer Michel de Nostredame was known for his gift of second sight. Traveling in Italy, he fell on his knees before a young Franciscan monk, calling him Holy Father. Forty years later that monk was elected Pope. Seer to French King Henri II and his wife Catherine de Médici, Nostradamus warned Henry that he would die in single combat

This 1920s photograph shows a fortune teller gazing into a crystal ball to reveal her client's destiny – a hazardous pastime as she could have been prosecuted under the Fraudulent Mediums Act.

when "In a cage of gold he will pierce his eyes. Two wounds one, then die a cruel death." The king was wounded in a jousting tournament. His opponent's lance pierced his eyes through the visor of his gilded helmet, a splinter entered his throat. As predicted, Henry died a lingering and painful death. Nostradamus also predicted the early demise of six of Henri and Catherine's children.

In a letter to his son Nostradamus tells how he would sit alone at night, entranced, gazing into a bowl of water on a brass tripod, lit by a candle. In the mirrored surface he would see visions – visions which reached forward over the next five centuries.

CRYSTALLOMANCY

Many crystals have been used for guidance. In ancient Greece, Axinomancers placed a piece of agate or jet onto a red hot ax to ascertain who the guilty party was in a crime – the crystal jumped to point at the person!

These days crystal divination packs such as The Crystal Wisdom Kit are available; or you can collect your own divining stones and make a suitable board to throw them on.

WHAT SCRYING CAN DO FOR YOU

Scrying can reveal what is to come. The accuracy of the vision depends on the skill of the seer. If the answer to a definite question is sought or greater insight needed into your life, then divining gems or crystal cards may be more effective than a crystal ball.

CRYSTAL BALLS

Crystal balls for gazing are traditionally gifted to you, but it is easy to purchase one in clear quartz, obsidian, smoky quartz, amethyst, and other crystals, or in glass crystal. All metaphysical or "New Age" retailers sell them and there are many crystal suppliers. You do not need a crystal; an ordinary mirror or a bowl of water can also be used .

BUYING A CRYSTAL BALL

Purchase your crystal ball when you are in a relaxed and receptive mood. Handle several balls. Feel how heavy they are, how comfortable you are with them. Look into them and see whether you prefer a perfectly plain sphere or one that has angles and planes within that may help you to see pictures. You will probably find yourself drawn to one crystal ball in particular, your eyes and hands will keep coming back to it. This is the ball for you.

HOW CRYSTAL BALLS WORK

When you gaze into a crystal ball you focus your intuition. Your rational mind no longer operates. Light reflects off the crystal, catching your eye and holding it firm. As your eyes go slightly out of focus, the crystal ball mists over. Within the mist, images form. The images are projected from within your own mind, but the crystal ball helps you to see them more clearly.

USING A CRYSTAL BALL

To crystal gaze you may want to have the room gently lit, or to use a strong light to reflect off the crystal. Some people like to use candlelight. When you are in a relaxed state, hold the ball for a few moments to attune it to your vibrations. Frame your question and consider possible solutions without giving them too much attention. Place the crystal ball on a black silk or velvet cloth. Focus gently on your crystal, and allow your eyes to go slightly out of focus. A mist will arise in the crystal and from within this mist, the images will form. Do not force them, let them arise naturally. Watch for pictures appearing either in the crystal or in your mind's eye. The meanings can be positive or negative. Write down what you see, even if it seems to be meaningless. If you persevere, you will understand. You may need to practice a few times before anything happens. Be patient and you will be rewarded.

You can also use the crystal ball as a focus for concentration, or as a meditation aid. Rather than looking for pictures or symbols, let the crystal enhance your intuition. Notice the feelings you have, the thoughts that come into your head, the insights that emerge about your life. The crystal can work on a very subtle level to guide you into a more fulfilled future.

Crystal balls can be made of clear quartz, obsidian, smoky quartz, amethyst, or glass crystal.

When in a relaxed state, hold the crystal ball in your hands for a few moments to attune it to your vibrations.

TRADITIONAL SYMBOLS

Image	Positive Interpretation	Negative Interpretation
Eye	Good luck	Bad luck
Moon	New growth	Disappointment
Star	Success	Warning
Globe	Travel	Standstill
Cat	Good luck	Trouble
Dog	Trustworthy friends	Deceitful friend
Snake	Learning	Betrayal
Bird	A message	Escapism
House	Well-being	Financial problems
Tree	Settling down	Loss
Wheel	Travel	Injury

(see also Dream Interpretation and Reading Tea Leaves)

KEEPING YOUR CRYSTAL BALL SAFE

Crystals easily pick up vibes from people or the environment – which is why, if you read for someone else, they need to cup their hands around the ball. To clear these vibes after use, you can place the ball under running water; visualize it surrounded with bright, white light; or spray it with Crystal Clear essence placed in a mister. The ball should then be wrapped in a silk or velvet cloth until needed.

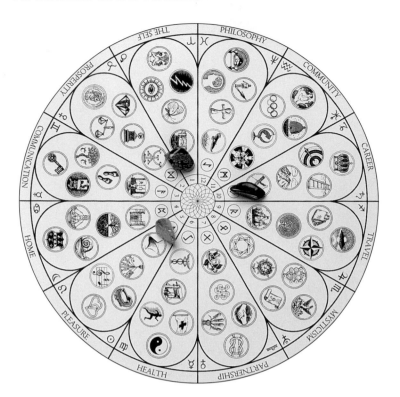

Crystals falling on the Crystal Wisdom Wheel show not only the energies that are operating, but also the sphere of life in which they will manifest.

CRYSTAL LAYOUTS

A handful of tumbled crystals can be used for crystal divination. The simplest way to work with them is to put them into a bag, shake them gently, ask your question, and take out the first two or three that your fingers touch. This will give you your answer. Before you look up the meaning, take time to gently focus on the crystal and see if the answer emerges spontaneously.

If you want to work with a more complex question or are looking for overall guidance, you can use Tarot layouts or a "year ahead" wheel. Retailers sell some excellent boards onto which you can throw your crystals. You then combine the answers on the board with the wisdom of the crystals.

CRYSTAL WISDOM

The Crystal Wisdom kit is a fun, easy-to-use system that works on various levels of consciousness. It combines the power of crystals with universal symbols and astrological wisdom, providing both healing and extraordinarily deep insights. While it can be used for divination,

having a useful Insight Wheel with clear, simple answers (see page 18); it can also be taken to a much deeper level. The originators, qualified crystal healers, created the pack specifically with the intention of awakening the user's intuitional gifts and to give a fresh perspective on life.

Within the pack are three casting wheels. The Life Wheel is divided into twelve "life areas."

CRYSTAL MEANINGS

Agate	Worldly success
Amethyst	Life changes and shift in consciousness
Black Agate	Courage and prosperity
Red Agate	Health and longevity
Aventurine	Growth and expansion
Blue Lace Agate	Healing needed
Citrine	Celestial wisdom
Diamond	Permanence
Emerald	Fertility
Hematite	New opportunities
Jade	Immortality and perfection
Red Jasper	Earthly affairs
Lapis Lazuli	Divine favor
Clear Quartz	Clarify issues
Rose Quartz	Love and self-healing
Ruby	Power and passion
Sapphire	Truth and chastity
Snowflake Obsidian	End of challenging time
Tiger's Eye	All is not as it seems
White Quartz	Profound changes
Unakite	Compromise and integration

Semiprecious stones can be substituted for gem stones, for example, clear quartz for diamond, garnet for ruby, peridot for emerald, and so on.

If your interest lies in Crystal Love or Crystal Abundance, consult the appropriate wheels for advice on how to proceed.

Each corresponds to a different aspect of life and contains symbols highlighting different facets of that area. The Healing Wheel consists of nineteen healing spheres, each one representing an aspect of the user's energy field – seven chakras, six realms of consciousness, five elements, and "All That Is." The Insight Wheel has ⌐ spheres offering messages such ⌐ "Hold back" for clear⌐ comprehen⌐ identifies⌐ nations⌐ interpretat⌐ Crystal Wi⌐

physical and spiritual vibratory fields. ⌐ these fields, information is passed to ⌐ that resonates on the same frequency, ⌐ in the crystals a vast library of knowl⌐ cards are designed to create a ⌐ with the user, so that the cards can ⌐ nd future life issues and guide a ⌐ growth. The cards also teach ⌐ crystals and can be used for ⌐ book accompanying the pack ⌐ ructions for healing, medi⌐ as well as interpretations ⌐ ssage they bring.

CRYSTAL

The creators o⌐ crystals are con⌐ ing spiritually j⌐ exist in a consta⌐

If Rose Quartz appears in your spread, Love is trying to make itself felt. It is time to open your heart chakra and allow more love into your life.

ELEMENTS

Crystal Ally cards are divided up into elements of Earth, Fire, Water, and Wind, which act rather like suits. In addition, the cards resonate with the various chakras. A reading with a preponderance of one of the elements and chakras indicates a specific lesson concerned with that area of life. This adds deeper layers of meaning to the reading. Each card has an appropriate spoken affirmation to change a pattern or integrate your expanded knowledge.

CRYSTAL ALLY

You need a large area in which to work with the cards – a big table top or generous floor space. The cards are shuffled and some of them can be reversed if appropriate. They are then spread out in a fan in front of you. You need to be in a meditative state to approach the cards, and a few good deep breaths will allow your body and mind to relax and become focused.

You must clearly formulate the issue that you wish to explore. While you hold that thought, your nondominant hand (usually the opposite hand to that with which you write) is placed about 2 inches (5 cm) above the cards. Moving slowly, the hand may become hot, tingle, or twitch. These phenomena are indications that the card beneath is appropriate. If the meaning of a particular card is unclear, then another card can be chosen to clarify or amplify the meaning.

REVERSED CARDS

Unlike Tarot and other cards, Crystal Ally cards do not have a separate or negative meaning if they are reversed. A reversed card indicates a deeper meaning, the greatest lesson, and an aspect of the current situation that you are having the greatest difficulty with. It can also indicate a blockage and a way of healing it.

When Zincite makes itself known, the creative energy is coming more strongly into your life.

ELEMENTAL ALLY

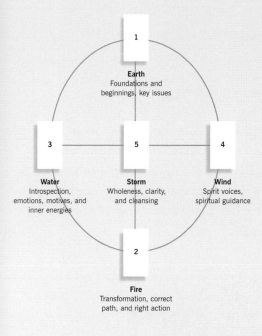

Earth
Foundations and beginnings, key issues

Water
Introspection, emotions, motives, and inner energies

Storm
Wholeness, clarity, and cleansing

Wind
Spirit voices, spiritual guidance

Fire
Transformation, correct path, and right action

THE PYRAMID

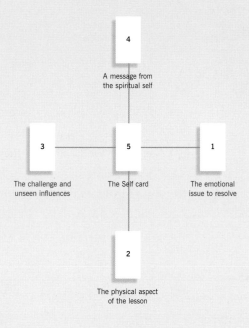

A message from the spiritual self

The challenge and unseen influences

The Self card

The emotional issue to resolve

The physical aspect of the lesson

THE CHAKRAS

Crown
Communication with the spiritual guide

Third Eye
Far sight, points to beliefs to be revaluated

Throat
How what you speak creates your life

Heart
Love and beauty

Solar Plexus
How your will is used

Navel
How you create experiences

Root
Physical experience

HEAVEN AND EARTH

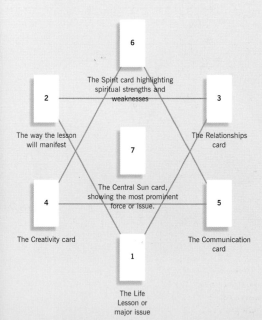

The Spirit card highlighting spiritual strengths and weaknesses

The way the lesson will manifest

The Relationships card

The Central Sun card, showing the most prominent force or issue.

The Creativity card

The Communication card

The Life Lesson or major issue

TRINITY SPREAD

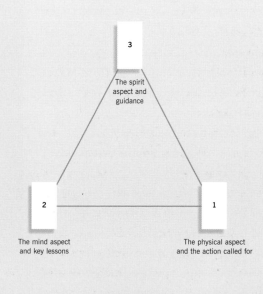

The spirit aspect and guidance

The mind aspect and key lessons

The physical aspect and the action called for

Reading Tea Leaves

Here thou, Great Anna! whom three realms obey,
Dost sometimes counsel take – and sometimes tea.
ALEXANDER POPE 1688–1744

When first introduced into Europe tea was an expensive luxury that few people could afford, and yet a tradition of fortune-telling by reading the leaves arose. Although tea leaf reading itself is not ancient, the tradition by which the leaves are read goes back into antiquity.

READING THE LEAVES

Tea was introduced into Europe in the seventeenth century and from there it traveled to the "New World"; but it had been drunk in India and the East for thousands of years. When tea first became available in the West, the price was so prohibitively high that it was beyond all but the very rich. For years, tea was so valued that it would be carefully dried out after use and reused by the servants, or sold again for a profit. It may have been this high value that made it so prized for domestic fortune-telling. By the time tea was freely available in Europe, every family had its own reader and the secret was passed from mother to daughter. In countries such as the Middle East where tea was not so freely drunk, coffee grounds would be used.

The art of "reading the leaves" (or reading from the dregs of a popular drink) was not new, however. In ancient Greece Kottavos was practiced. The dregs of wine would be thrown into a metal bowl. The shape formed from the splash of liquid and sediment was read as an omen. Understanding the shapes came down through

history into the twentieth century. In England, the increasing popularity of tea bags led to tea-leaf reading becoming redundant, but it flourished elsewhere.

Patterns in the leaves show up most clearly against a white porcelain cup. Turn the cup slowly, looking at the images from all sides. Note where they lie within the cup.

*The position of the leaves
in the cup indicates
the timing of events.*

WHAT TEA LEAVES CAN DO FOR YOU

Tea-leaf reading can be fun. Trying to ascertain the shapes, allowing the imagination free reign, is an enjoyable pastime for a lazy afternoon. But the level of divination is light: It is more likely that the tall, dark stranger you see riding into your life will turn out to be the new mailman, than the object of a true oracle of love.

DIVINING BY THE CUP

You should use good quality loose-leaf tea. Cheap tea is small-leaved and does not form clear pictures. The tea should be brewed in a pot with a wide spout and poured unstrained into a white china cup. The cup needs to be wide and bowl-like – breakfast cups are ideal. Mugs with perpendicular sides are not suitable.

Drink the tea until half an inch (1.5 cm) remains in the bottom. The cup is then quickly swirled around and inverted over the saucer. When all the liquid has drained off, the cup can be turned upright again.

READING THE CUP

Contemplate the cup quietly, allowing the imagination full play. Do not force the pictures to emerge, and do not expect them to be too graphic. They usually suggest themselves rather than being clearly seen. Features that stand out clearly are more important than those that are vague. If a cup is muddled and indistinct, it probably reflects the state of mind of the enquirer.

THE SHAPE OF THINGS TO COME

Pictures close to the top of the cup indicate immediate events; those halfway down are up to three months away, while those at the bottom relate to the distant future. A number next to a symbol can indicate timing and a letter suggests the name of a person. The handle indicates the enquirer. The space next to the handle corresponds with the home, so pictures close to the handle are close to home. Pictures opposite the handle relate to outsiders. The bottom of the cup is a place of sadness or ill fortune, the top one of joy. To the left of the handle are opportunities or events that have been thrown away, to the right are present or future events. Dark leaves can indicate men or dark people, light leaves women or pale people.

Serpentine lines indicate a pathway. Surrounded by dots at the top of a cup, they can indicate money or a long life. At the bottom, or surrounded by clouds, they indicate reverses. Circles indicate completion, wavy lines uncertainty, straight lines a direct course. Dashes indicate a project that needs time to mature. A cross within a circle can indicate enforced detention in a hospital or a prison.

Top of cup: Joy

To left of handle: Past

Handle: Enquirer

At handle: Home

Opposite handle: Outsiders

Top of cup: Immediate future

Middle of cup: 3 months

Base of cup: Distant

To right of handle: Present or future

Base of cup: Sadness

THE SYMBOLS

(POSITIVE OR NEGATIVE ACCORDING TO POSITION IN CUP)

Acorn

Plenty, health

Aircraft

New projects, elevation

Anchor

Journey, rest

Angel

Good news

Arrow

Unpleasant news

Baby

New interests

Ball and chain

Commitments

Basket

Gift

Bear

Foreign lands

Bees

Industry

Bell

Marriage

Birds

Good news

Boat

Discovery

Book

Revelation

Boot

Caution

Broom

Clearing out

Butterfly

Innocent pleasure

Cat

Treachery

Clock

Sickness

Clouds

Doubts

Clover

Luck

Coffin

Death, loss

Cow

Prosperity

Crown

Honor

Daffodil

Acquisition of wealth

Dagger

Danger

Dog

True Friends

Donkey

Patience

Drum

Quarrels

Egg

Increase

Eye

Inspect carefully

Fan

Flirtation

Fish

Lucky speculation

Flag

Danger

Flock

Sudden gathering

Flowers

Celebration

Heart

Romance

Horse

A Lover

Fox or Hare

Sagacity, foresight.

Key

Enlightenment

Kite

Direction

Ladder

Advancement

Letter

News

Lion

Powerful friends

Mountains

Obstacles

Mouse

Poverty or theft

Purse

Loss or gain

Owl

Trouble

Ring

Proposal

Scales

Justice

Scissors

Separation

Ship

Increase

Spider

Subterfuge

Star

Hope

Sun

Happiness

Van/Horse and Cart

Movement

Volcano

Passion

Web

Deceit

Cartomancy

The oldest theory behind cartomancy is that a mystic power of Fate guides the shuffling and dealing of the cards, so the resulting layout will yield a meaningful message when properly interpreted.

BARBARA WALKER

Cartomancy is the art of using cards for divination. It began with Tarot cards, and the ordinary deck of fifty-two playing cards can be used in the same way. It is usual to purchase a new pack of cards and to keep these exclusively for divination.

Playing cards have been used for divination for at least four hundred years.

TRADITIONAL SYMBOLISM

Cards have been used for divination for much longer than they have for games of chance. Playing cards developed out of the Tarot. The Minor Arcana became the four suits – Hearts, Diamonds, Clubs, and Spades. The only one of the Major Arcana cards to find its way into the playing card pack was the Fool, which is now known as the Joker. Like all other methods of divination, playing cards use symbols to represent archetypes, experiences, and people, as expressed through various aspects of life. The suits have particular "traits" and are associated with different personalities.

USING PLAYING CARDS FOR DIVINATION

Playing cards can be used in much the same way as the Tarot and there are additional spreads that are particularly suited to the symbolism of playing cards. The reader focuses on the question during the initial shuffling and the cards are then cut twice toward the reader, using the left hand.

The reader gathers the three heaps together to form one pile in the center of the table before laying out and interpreting the spread. If the spread has a predominance of Clubs, then the reading relates to practical or business affairs; Diamonds indicate financial affairs; Hearts emotional and romantic matters; and Spades pinpoint challenges to come.

WHAT PLAYING CARDS CAN DO FOR YOU

Playing cards can be used to forecast the future, examining the influences that will be brought to bear on your life in the near future or in the year ahead. In the hands of a skilled reader, they can be used to answer specific questions and may well illuminate underlying trends or aspects of your life that have not yet come to your attention. As certain cards represent people, they can indicate someone who is coming into, or passing out of, your life. The cards may well hint at a relationship to come or perhaps describe a prospective partner.

THE SUITS

In divination with playing cards the emphasis is on the subtle variations that come through the effect of a suit on, say, an Ace. So, the Ace of Hearts is concerned with home and domestic happiness while the Ace of Clubs represents success, wealth, and renown in the outside world. The Ace of Diamonds may mean money is coming, or an engagement; but the Ace of Spades has traditionally been known as the "death card" and may indicate quarrels or the breakup of a relationship. While the ten is a lucky card in most suits, the ten of Spades is an inauspicious card.

DIAMONDS stand for money and material possessions, business affairs, status, and ecurity needs. This pragmatic suit can indicate unfinished business and show where more effort may be needed. It represents very pale, fair-haired people, usually with light blue eyes; and those who are sophisticated and self-assured.

HEARTS is the emotional suit, relating to romance, kindness, and an affectionate, sympathetic nature. This suit may well indicate marriage, children, and artistic pursuits. However, it can relate to emotional stress when adversely affected. It represents people with light brown or auburn hair, and blue, hazel, or gray eyes.

CLUBS relate to prestige, enterprise, and influence; and an active, energetic personality. This suit represents people with dark brown hair and eyes, often with a high color. Clubs in a reading can to some extent, offset less positive cards.

SPADES have traditionally been regarded as heralds of misfortune. Yet they provide a timely warning as well as signifying possible conflict. This suit is related to mental activities, law and order, and foreign affairs. It represents powerful, influential people with strong characters; and those with sallow complexions and very dark hair and eyes.

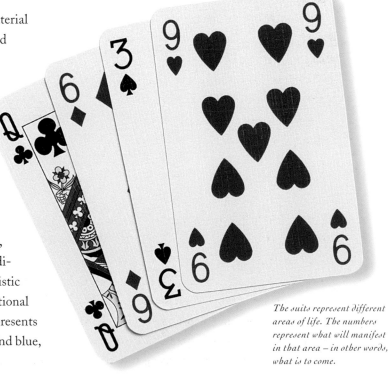

The suits represent different areas of life. The numbers represent what will manifest in that area – in other words, what is to come.

89

INTERPRETING THE CARDS

The symbolism of playing cards is complex and, for the Court cards, may depend on the sex of the enquirer. The meanings of the corresponding Minor Arcana can be used. Books such as *Card Fortune-Telling* by Charles Thorp (Foulshams) give detailed interpretations.

LAYOUTS

While all of the spreads featured in this book can be used with playing cards, there are some additional ones that give excellent results.

THE MYSTIC PYRAMID

This spread develops themes from past influences that have a bearing on the present situation or question (the bottom row) up to the outcome of the action (the apex of the pyramid), and indicates a complex causal chain interweaving its way through the cards. It is particularly useful when you want to explore a situation in great depth. When the intuition of the reader has been finely honed so that inconsistent factors can be weighed up and the most important recognized, and when the reader is thoroughly familiar with the cards, the result can be a highly individual reading.

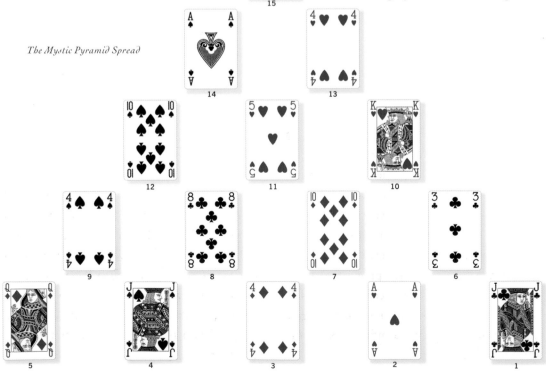

The Mystic Pyramid Spread

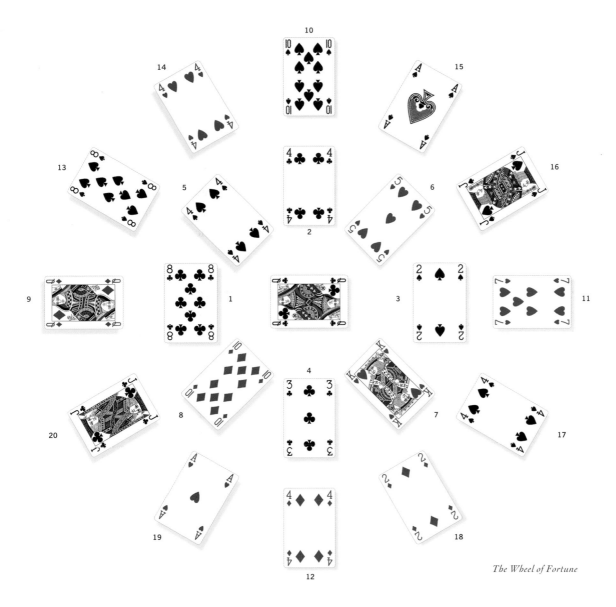

The Wheel of Fortune

To lay out the mystic pyramid, thoroughly shuffle the cards and then deal the top fifteen cards face up starting with a row of five cards, then four, then three, then two, and finally one. You begin your interpretation with card fifteen, and follow its antecedents down through cards thirteen and fourteen. As you progress, each card gathers import from the two cards below it. The card placed at position eleven is often very significant. It shows helpful or harmful influences that affect the whole edifice.

THE WHEEL OF FORTUNE

The Wheel of Fortune uses pairings of cards, which must be weighed up and judged, as some will conflict and others strengthen each other. The reading progresses from the rim of the wheel toward the center, rather as though peeling off layers of meaning until the core is reached. The cards are laid out as shown above around a significator card chosen from the King or Queen of a suit appropriate to the question and questioner.

Angelic Messages

The angel went in and said to her, "Greetings favored one! The Lord is with you."

Angels have been announcing future events since time immemorial. These messengers of God appear on temple walls in Egypt, Persia, Turkey, India, Sumeria, Babylon, Greece, and South America. Their words are in holy books of Judaism, Islam, Christianity, Hinduism, and Buddhism, as well as in contemporary writings. Many religions believe that we each have our own guardian angel.

ANGELIC PRESENCES

Angels are concerned with prophecy and miraculous events. The Koran was dictated to Mohammed by Gabriel, the Angel of Knowledge and Revelation. Gabriel, one of the best-known angelic messengers appears in the Gospel of Luke. First, he tells Zechariah, a temple priest, that his wife Elizabeth will conceive a son in her old age. When Zechariah doubts this, he is struck dumb until the words are proved true. Then Gabriel goes to Mary to tell her that, in her case, even the conception will be miraculous, with "the Holy Spirit coming upon her."

In Matthew's Gospel, an angel appears to Joseph to reassure him he should marry the pregnant Mary, to whom he is betrothed. Angels later warn Joseph to flee into Egypt. When Jesus goes into the wilderness, angels attend him. When the women go to Jesus' tomb, an angel of the Lord, whose face shines like lightning, descends from heaven, rolls away the stone from the door, sits himself down on it, and announces the resurrection.

ANGELIC APPEARANCE

Throughout history, angels either appear in human form, maybe with a shining countenance; or as winged beings, balls of light, voices, or other mysterious apparitions. Nowadays, angels may make their presence known by sight, smell, color, or an inner knowing.

ANGELIC INTENTION

Angels are intermediaries between God and humankind. They are closest to earth and can minister to human needs. They can also take humans into heavenly realms, and show them the future. The seven archangels of the Angels Tarot, Michael, Gabriel, Raphael, Uriel, Raguel, Remiel, and Sariel oversee this process and have their own specific responsibilities.

ACCESSING ANGELS

Angelic teachers are accessible through your own intuition. The more you can develop this, and the more you learn to listen to your own inner voices, the clearer the guidance will be. There are many packs on the market to aid this process.

Seraphim
(Love)

Cherubim
(Wisdom)

Thrones
(Chariots of God)

Dominos
(Nature)

Virtues
(Miracles)

Powers
(Protection)

Principalities
(Karma of Nations)

Archangels
(Liaison with God)

Angels
(Ministers)

THE ANGELS TAROT

Based on a Tarot pack, The Angels Tarot incorporates angelic messengers into the Major Arcana. The Minor Arcana, stylized cherubs, have the same meanings as in Tarot.

HOW TO USE THE ANGELS TAROT

The cards can be used for meditation, during which you ask your own personal angelic guides to reveal the mysteries contained in the cards. They can also be used with classic Tarot spreads or a layout specially created for the deck.

WHAT THE ANGELS TAROT CAN DO FOR YOU

Working with this deck invites the presence of angels into your life. The angels work with you through the cards and the insights you receive. As your intuitive response to the cards grows, so your attunement with the angels deepens. The creators of the cards suggest that you should ask for a special "Tarot Angel" to oversee your work with the cards.

THE CELESTIAL LADDER

1 Mundane affairs and relationships
2 Higher self, spiritual progress, aspirations
3 Karmic issues
4 Shadow side, inner demons, fears
5 Inner power, strength, and virtues
6 Health and vitality
7 Creativity
8 Spiritual wisdom and insight
9 Ability to love unconditionally

(see left)

THE MAJOR ARCANA

1 **Adamel** *The Fool Who Attained Knowledge:* Start of the spiritual journey and the unrealized end

2 **Abraras** *Angel of Magic:* The ability to take the spiritual and manifest it in the material

3 **Gabriel** *Angel of Revelation:* Threshold of the mysteries, revealing of answers

4 **Mary** *Queen of Angels:* Quickening of endeavors

5 **Metatron** *King of Angels:* Grounding and stabilizing influences

6 **Raphael** *Angel of Healing:* Knowledge and healing

7 **Theliel** *Prince of Lovers:* Fulfilling love or unbalanced relationship

8 **Cherubiel** *Chief of Charioteers:* Need for skill and alertness to keep on path

8 **Michael** *Champion of Justice:* Truth is invincible

10 **Orifiel** *Angel of Wilderness:* Time to pause and reflect

11 **Manu** *Angel of Fate:* Nothing stays the same

12 **Fortitude** *Angel of Strength:* Inner strength

13 **Uzza** *Hung between Heaven and Earth:* A fall or a loss

14 **Abaddon** *Angel of Death:* The end of a phase

15 **Temperance** *Angel of Time:* Birth of a new cycle

16 **Satan** *Prince of Darkness:* Do not be imprisoned by instincts

17 **Barakiel** *Lightning of God:* A breakthrough or creative insight

18 **Anael** *Angel of the Star of Love:* Development of unconditional love

19 **Moon** *Angel of Dreams:* Time for rest and reflection

20 **Uriel** *Regent of the Sun:* Enlightenment and illumination

21 **Jeremiel** *Herald of Judgment:* Time of reckoning and resurrection

22 **Shekinah** *Soul of the World:* Achievement and culmination of goals

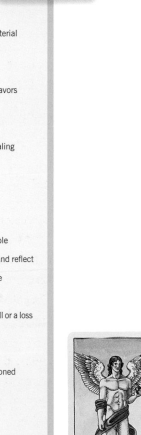

Mary
Queen of Angels

Queen of Hearts

Adamel
The Fool Who Attained Knowledge

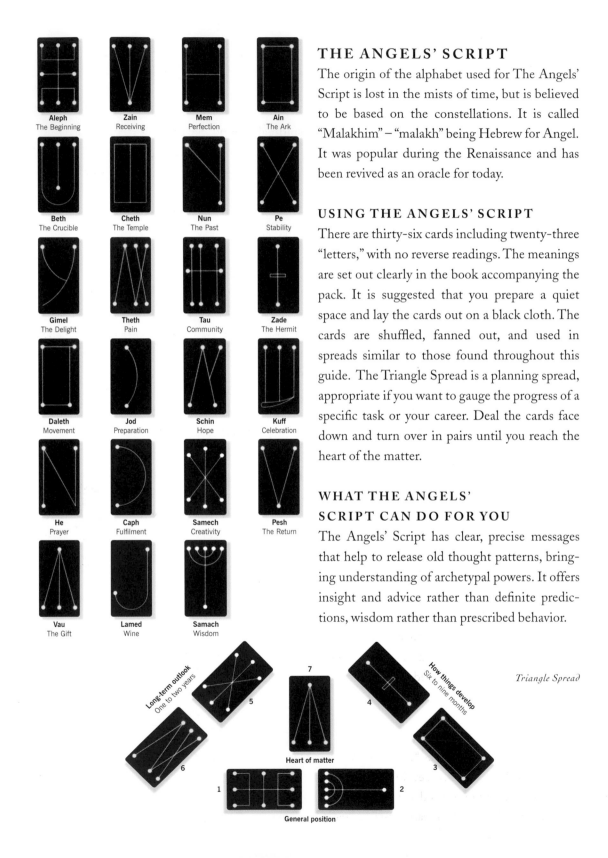

Aleph
The Beginning

Zain
Receiving

Mem
Perfection

Ain
The Ark

Beth
The Crucible

Cheth
The Temple

Nun
The Past

Pe
Stability

Gimel
The Delight

Theth
Pain

Tau
Community

Zade
The Hermit

Daleth
Movement

Jod
Preparation

Schin
Hope

Kuff
Celebration

He
Prayer

Caph
Fulfilment

Samech
Creativity

Pesh
The Return

Vau
The Gift

Lamed
Wine

Samach
Wisdom

THE ANGELS' SCRIPT

The origin of the alphabet used for The Angels' Script is lost in the mists of time, but is believed to be based on the constellations. It is called "Malakhim" – "malakh" being Hebrew for Angel. It was popular during the Renaissance and has been revived as an oracle for today.

USING THE ANGELS' SCRIPT

There are thirty-six cards including twenty-three "letters," with no reverse readings. The meanings are set out clearly in the book accompanying the pack. It is suggested that you prepare a quiet space and lay the cards out on a black cloth. The cards are shuffled, fanned out, and used in spreads similar to those found throughout this guide. The Triangle Spread is a planning spread, appropriate if you want to gauge the progress of a specific task or your career. Deal the cards face down and turn over in pairs until you reach the heart of the matter.

WHAT THE ANGELS' SCRIPT CAN DO FOR YOU

The Angels' Script has clear, precise messages that help to release old thought patterns, bringing understanding of archetypal powers. It offers insight and advice rather than definite predictions, wisdom rather than prescribed behavior.

Triangle Spread

Long-term outlook
One to two years

How things develop
Six to nine months

7

5

4

Heart of matter

6

3

1

2

General position

ANGELIC MESSENGER CARDS

The Angelic Messenger Cards are unique in that they combine the wisdom of the angels with the beauty and symbolism of flowers to awaken your spirit's light, create loving relationships, support your life choices, and heal and balance your body, mind, and spirit.

THE TRANSCENDENT QUALITY OF FLOWERS

According to the creator of Angelic Messenger Cards, flowers are angels talking to you. Each flower reflects a heavenly teacher. Flowers show you that you have something unique to contribute to life. Working with the guidance of the angels helps you to feel love more intensely for all things. As you treasure the beauty of the flowers, so you will discover the buried treasure of your own soul.

USING THE CARDS

The cards are designed as a "living prayer" to help you resolve problems, develop inner trust, affirm yourself, and renew and awaken the spiritual energy of love. You can draw a "daily guidance" card for specific concerns or simply as an attunement, or you can use the specially designed spreads.

The cards reflect six aspects of love (or spiritual energy). Seven cards relate to each one of these aspects: Reflection (1–7), Partnership (8–14), Integration (15–21), Alignment (22–8), Rejuvenation (29–35), and Nourishment (36–42). In addition, there are four Wild Cards of Divine Guidance to help you perceive the spiritual encounter that is waiting to emerge in your life. If you draw one of these cards, it is a response to your prayers or seeking. It alerts you to a situation, event, or breakthrough opportunity that is coming your way. Finally, there are two Wild Cards of Abundance to alert you to impending opportunities for abundance and aid you in evaluating your decisions by spiritual criteria.

WHAT THE ANGELIC MESSENGER CARDS CAN DO FOR YOU

Angelic Messenger Cards are designed to help you reconnect to your angelic teachers and your own spiritual roots. These connections bring serenity and self-realization, and enhance your creative vision.

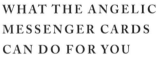

ANGEL BLESSINGS

Angel Blessings is a new look at the hierarchy of angels, and the cards are used in a sacramental way, invoking the loving presence of angels. This spiritually based pack is designed to help you to remember your divine identity, who you really are, and why you are here.

THE ANGELIC HIERARCHY

In this pack, each angel has an attribute to share with you; and the unique qualities of each angel blend with those of other angels. In this respect the angels are like a large, extended family.

Within that family are Orders, each Great Archangel being a primary expression of a quality, the angels expressing different facets of the quality. So, the First Order angels have heart-centered activities in common; the Second Order, the outward expression of inner qualities; and the Third Order, emotional depth

44 ~ Cerviel

Courage

Cerviel, Angel of Courage, helps you clear away obstructions in time of crisis and loosens your resistance to necessary change.

26 ~ Nathaniel

Fire

Nathaniel, Angel of Fire, helps you to burn away misconceptions and self limitations. He increases energy flow, allowing kundalini energy to rise.

33 ~ Hamied

Miracles

Hamied, Angel of Miracles, has the mission of sparking the memory of your own innate divinity and bringing a miracle into your life.

25 ~ Galgaliel

Vibration

Galgaliel, Angel of Vibration,
watches over your emotional
vibrations and helps to bring
you the fire of soul love that
frees you from illusion.

28 ~ Charmiene

Harmony

Charmiene, Angel of Harmony,
enfolds you in a gentle mantle
of self-love and acceptance,
enabling you to integrate the
opposites within you.

23 ~ Zagzagel

Wisdom

Zagzagel, Angel of Wisdom,
awakens your ability to receive
wisdom from within and to attune
to divine guidance.

21 ~ Iofiel

Beauty

Iofiel, Angel of Beauty, helps
you to see the beauty within
the material world and to radiate
your own inner divinity.

and power. The Golden Light Order balances them all – and shines a light on what you don't want to see.

Within the Orders are powerful Great Archangels, who have sent fragments of themselves to Earth. The humans who carry these fragments feel that they have a mission in life that the cards will reveal. Lesser Archangels bring joy to life and create group relationships.

USING THE CARDS

Begin by selecting an Angel of the Day and meditating with this. This helps to deepen your attunement not only to the card but also to the feeling, gift, and challenge it embodies. The cards can then be used in special Sacraments (spreads).

WHAT ANGEL BLESSINGS CAN DO FOR YOU

This is a very spiritually based pack and its language is that of love with religious undertones. It is nondenominational but was written by an ordained minister. If you want to deepen your attunement to universal love and work much more closely with angelic forces, then this pack helps you to recognize the habits and beliefs that prevent you from receiving love and opening your life to be an expression of divine energy.

Throwing the Dice

I have set my life upon a cast
And I will stand the hazard of the die
SHAKESPEARE: RICHARD III

Dice are a traditional tool for fortune-telling found all over the world. Used for casting lots, dice are an indication of fate. Used for games of chance, they provide an opportunity for Lady Luck to shine on the fortunate. Dice have the advantage of being highly portable.

THE DIE IS CAST

The saying "the die is cast" comes from the use of dice, or a die, for divination or to indicate fate. It can be argued that throwing the dice is one of the most ancient of all systems of divination. And lots have long been cast to allot property – as when Christ's robe was given to a soldier on the throw of a dice.

The oldest known gaming boards come from the royal tombs of Ur, dating back to 3000 BCE. Six pyramidal dice were used. In nearby ancient Egypt, throwsticks were used, from which dice were later developed. Throwsticks were made from reed, ivory, or wood. One side, left undecorated, was slightly concave. The convex side would be engraved or carved. Thrown at random in groups of six or so, they would be read according to which side faced up.

Mercury (otherwise known as Hermes) was the divine patron of dice-players. Call on him to help the dice fall for maximum clarification of an issue.

Throwing dice into a circle is one of the oldest forms of divination. Disregard a die that falls outside the circle.

In ancient Greece, knuckle bones were used. These bones, which came from the hooves of goats and sheep were naturally four-sided. Many other ancient peoples used these bones in the same way. In some cultures the sides were filed flat and symbols incised upon them. The Greeks, however, left them in their natural state as each of the four faces was different – one concave, one convex, another almost flat, and the fourth irregular. Dice were also manufactured specifically for gaming purposes. As the use of dice became more sophisticated, dice were made from crystal, amber, pottery, and ivory. Squatting figures modeled in silver have been found, with numbers on different parts of their body, which were used in a similar way to square dice.

A DIVINE PATRON

The Roman god Mercury was the patron of dice-players. Mercury had the gift of prophecy and used his dice for divination as well as gaming. The sheep and goats out of which the dice were made were also considered to be sacred to Mercury by the Romans.

By 1400 BCE dice had taken on the appearance with which we are familiar today. The faces were arranged so that the spots on opposite sides always added up to 7.

WHAT DICE CAN DO FOR YOU

Dice give a simplistic answer to a question, unless the complex question-and-answer method is used. They are purely intended for fortune-telling rather than to give an insight into a situation.

TWELVE HOUSES
HOROSCOPE WHEEL

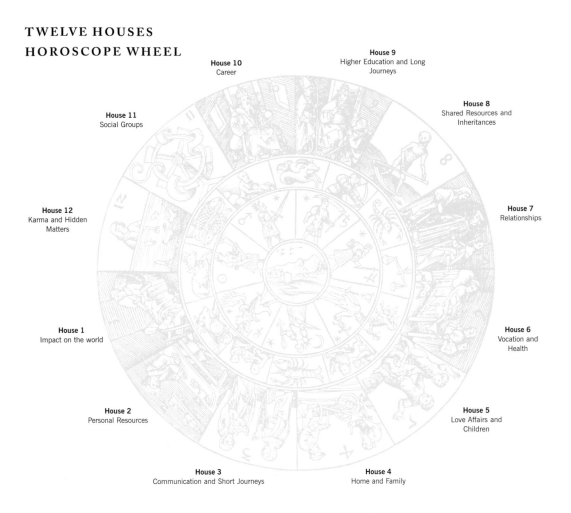

House 10
Career

House 9
Higher Education and Long Journeys

House 8
Shared Resources and Inheritances

House 11
Social Groups

House 7
Relationships

House 12
Karma and Hidden Matters

House 6
Vocation and Health

House 1
Impact on the world

House 5
Love Affairs and Children

House 2
Personal Resources

House 3
Communication and Short Journeys

House 4
Home and Family

DICING ANCIENT AND MODERN

There are ancient systems of fortune-telling with dice that require set questions and long lists of possible answers. Such lists are still available in books today. Another system, which is more modern, uses three colors of dice – red, green, and white. Because each color has a different meaning and its own symbol for each number, the combination of possible answers is much greater (216 permutations). So, too, is the list of meanings, and in this case a book is needed to understand all the implications.

USING DICE

The simplest method of fortune-telling with dice takes two or three dice and a large circle marked out on the ground. You hold the dice cupped in

your hand while focusing on the question. The dice are lightly shaken and allowed to fall onto the circle. Any dice that fall outside the circle are discarded. (If all the dice fall outside the circle, this is said to be an indication of estrangement. The dice should be thrown again. If they once more fall outside the circle, then no fortune can be read that day.) The numbers on the top face of the dice in the circle are added together and the meaning is read.

A somewhat complex, but more comprehesive, version divides the circle into twelve sections. (These sections correspond to the twelve houses of the horoscope.) The meaning of the dice is then read against the background of the matters relating to the "house," the section(s) of the circle into which they fall.

DIVINATORY MEANINGS

1 Singleness

1 can be loneliness or loss. It can also be an individual, whole and unique.

2 Partnership

2 can indicate love but it can also signal infatuation. The partnership may be a business one. There is usually success with 2 but it may follow much work.

3 Celebration

3 indicates a pleasant surprise. It is a sign of good news, the fulfilment of a wish or of joy to come.

4 Security

4 is a sign of putting down roots, of finding a secure base. It can indicate a need for recuperation or recharging your energies. In some systems, 4 indicates an unpleasant surprise.

5 Conflict

5 can indicate arguments or losses. It may warn of an illness to come. 5 may also indicate an influential meeting with a stranger.

6 Change

6 may indicate a move into a new situation or being pulled back into a past situation. In some systems, 6 indicates the loss of something you value.

7 Growth

7 can indicate that you are moving forward, albeit slowly. The end of confusion is in sight. 7 may also warn of scandal.

8 Reckoning

With 8 the past may catch up with you. It is time to right a previous wrong. 8 can also indicate that it is time for a new job or a change of environment, around which there may be some worry or stress.

9 Commitment

9 may indicate a wedding in the near future or a period of happy family life. It can also indicate money coming, a comfortable situation, a period of satisfaction.

10 Success

10 may indicate advancement in business but it can indicate success in all things – especially health, money, and love.

11 News

This may indicate the death of someone you know, but the news may also be good. 11 often signifies a minor event that leads to greater things.

12 Travel

You may travel or receive visitors from overseas. A new form of transportation is possible. Under 12, you may well receive an important letter.

13 Luck – good or bad

Traditionally an unlucky number, 13 may indicate bad news. On the other hand, it can indicate the help of a woman with influence.

14 Opportunity

Under 14 you may find a new admirer or receive the help of an influential person.

15 New beginnings

You may need to exercise caution when you receive 15 since it can indicate trouble brewing but on the whole it is favorable.

16 Happiness

You may find yourself in a successful partnership or undertaking an enjoyable journey.

17 Profit

17 can indicate a profitable contact from abroad but it can also point to a successful love affair. Career prospects may cause concern, but this will pass.

18 Fulfillment

18 can indicate great good fortune, promotion, or happiness in love.

Bottlebrush
Callistemon linearis

*To let go and cope with change.
Mother/child bonding.*

Dowsing

All information is available to us at some level depending on our attunement.

DAWN ROBINS

Dowsing has been in use for thousands of years. Traditionally, hazel twigs divined water and precious minerals. A wedding ring tied to a thread has been spun to sex an unborn child for hundreds of years. Nowadays metal rods are freely available and pendulums come in all shapes and sizes.

DOWSING THE FUTURE

Dowsers are diviners, practitioners of a sacred art, and were regarded with awe and respect for hundreds of years. It is a gift that frequently passed down through families, often peasants or herders who would use it to find water for their animals. Being able to divine water in the desert was much valued, for instance. Many of the Celtic, Byzantine, and other early Christian saints were dowsers. Stories tell of how they struck a rock and a spring flowed – and, frequently, is still flowing today. Such springs were regarded as sacred, possessed of healing powers.

Although dowsing could also be used to ascertain the future, this was one of its lesser uses. Other methods were favored. This may well be because the answer you get from dowsing the future is a probability at best unless you are very skilled. The future is not always fixed and dowsing is open to influence. The answer you receive may be the answer you want to hear rather than what will actually happen. So it may be better to ask someone else to dowse on your behalf.

WHAT DOWSING CAN DO FOR YOU

Dowsing usually gives a clear yes-or-no answer. It is particularly useful for establishing what you need. You can write a list of possibilities, for instance, run your finger down it and stop when it says yes (helpful for choosing remedies, oils, and testing for food allergies). You can also look back into the past – many people use a dowsed time of birth for their astrology chart, for example, when they do not know the exact time. It may help you to find suitable places or things that are lost – but this depends on whether your subconscious knows the answer. If it does not, you will not find what you lost.

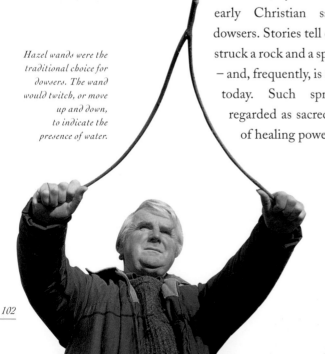

Hazel wands were the traditional choice for dowsers. The wand would twitch, or move up and down, to indicate the presence of water.

Kapok Bush
Cochlospermum fraseri

Perseverance and willing

Silver Princess
Eucalyptus caesia

Life direction and purpose.

Sturt Desert Rose
Gossypium sturtianum

True to self.
Releases guilt.

The Australian Bush Flower essences are gentle, vibratory remedies for physical, emotional, mental, and spiritual well-being. You can choose the right essence by allowing yourself to be intuitively attracted to a flower, or you can put your finger on each card in turn and dowse with a pendulum for the appropriate one for you.

BODY DOWSING

Some people feel strong sensations in their body which give them an answer. It can feel like being "kicked" in the stomach, or getting an electric shock, or your body might twitch or jerk. This is useful when finding things.

You can also use muscle testing. If you have someone to help you, ask them to stand in front of you and put one hand on your left shoulder. Put your right arm out straight at shoulder height. Ask your dowsing partner to say "Resist" and press down on your right wrist. Your arm should stay straight. If you touch the part of your body where there is a problem, when you try to resist your arm will go down. Hold the correct remedy over the part and it will stay strong (if checking vitamin supplements, flower essences, etc., hold them over your solar plexus.

If you are dowsing a "yes/no" question you can use your hands. Hold your right thumb and fore-finger together. Place your left thumb and forefinger through the "loop." When you ask your question, pull with the left hand. If the loop holds, the answer is "yes." If it pulls apart, the answer is "no."

USING DOWSING

To divine well the mind has to be clear. Clarity of intention, focus, and trust are essential, as is a correctly phrased question. If you are not getting a clear answer it could well be that you are not asking exactly the right question. You need to be precise and avoid ambiguity. Having asked your question, it is important not to keep checking. Trust is essential. If you are unsure of the answer, you can try a different method of divination but do not keep asking until you receive the answer you like! The answer may not yet be settled, in which case the rod or pendulum will reflect the uncertainty, by refusing to move at all or by behaving in a very erratic fashion.

The body has its own way of answering questions. If the thumb and finger hold, the answer is yes!

PRACTICALITIES

Traditionally, hazel twigs were used for dowsing. Copper rods also did the same job. Nowadays you can buy rods or make your own from wire coat hangers. These are useful if you want to trace water or other things in the ground over which you are walking. The rods are held loosely in your hands, pointing forward. They twitch, open, or cross when you reach your goal. However, you need to be specific. "Show me water" will show you water whether it is running in a small pipe or a huge underground spring, and the rods will twitch at other energies.

Using a pendulum is a much easier way to dowse questions. Hold the chain about 3–4 inches (7–10 cm) above the pendulum. Establish "yes" and "no" by programing these in as diagonals – one direction for "yes," another for "no." Swing the pendulum in the direction for "yes" a few times, telling yourself: "This is yes." Then program "no" to go in another diagonal. If the pendulum "wobbles" this answer is probably "maybe/undecided" but check this out.

Deliberately swing your pendulum in the "yes" and then the "no" direction until you have programed in, and can instantly recognize, these two responses in answer to questions.

If you are not focused enough, or if you have not phrased your question correctly, the pendulum will return to neutral or the energy will go out of the swing – in which case check whether it is the right time to ask and whether you have phrased the question correctly. Before starting a dowsing session it is usual to check if it is right to dowse and ask that the dowsing be for the highest good of all concerned.

To time events, or to ascertain dates, etc., dowse over numbers written in a semi-circle. The pendulum will point to the answer. Here it is between three and four. The answer could be March–April, around 3.15, or whatever is relevant to your question.

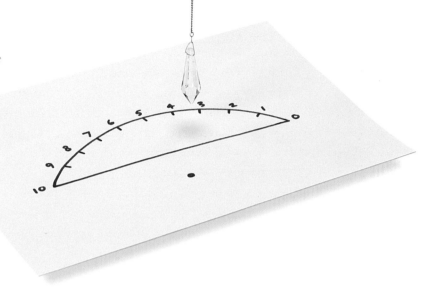

TIMING

Draw a semicircle on a piece of paper. Write 0 at one end and 10 at the other. The pendulum will swing toward the correct number. If you want to work with numbers higher than ten, ask the pendulum if it is greater than ten, twenty, thirty etc., and you will get a yes-or-no answer. Then use the numbers in the semicircle to refine the answer.

You can ask ages, dates, or times in this way. The more energy the swing has, the more important the answer.

MAP DOWSING

You can use a map or plan to dowse. This is helpful if you want to find something you have lost, choose a place to go on holiday, or plan a move. It can also be used to place beneficial crystals for maximum effect. Simply hold the pendulum over the map and move it around slowly in a grid. The "yes" swing of the pendulum will become stronger as you near the correct/appropriate spot. You must hold a clear intent and strong picture of what you want to know to be successful.

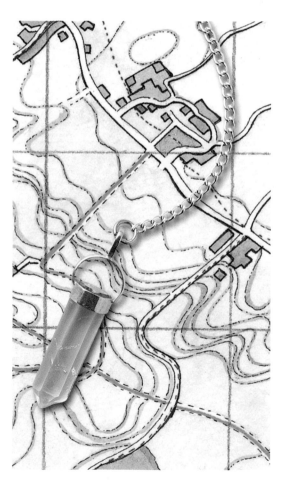

Dream Interpretation

> There is some ill a-brewing towards my rest
> For I did dream of money-bags tonight.
>
> **SHAKESPEARE: THE MERCHANT OF VENICE**

Oniromancy, the study of dreams, goes way back into prehistory. Dreams were valued as messages from the gods (or God) and many ancient temples had rooms set aside for healing or prophetic dreams. To those skilled in interpretation, the future was revealed. Today, anyone can understand dreams.

BIBLICAL DREAMS

Dreams played a great part in biblical life. In Genesis we are told of Joseph a younger, much-loved son whose eleven brothers hated him. One day, Joseph went to his brothers and said: "Listen to this dream I have had. We were in the field binding sheaves, and my sheaf rose on end and stood upright, and your sheaves gathered round and bowed low before my sheaf." Later he told his brothers of another dream he had: "The sun and moon and eleven stars were bowing down to me." (*Genesis 37*)

The furious brothers sold Joseph into slavery in Egypt, where he prospered for a time but was eventually thrown into prison. Here he met Pharaoh's chief butler and baker who had angered their master. The butler dreamt of a vine on which three branches budded, blossomed, and ripened into grapes immediately. The butler held Pharaoh's cup, picked the grapes, crushed them, and put the cup into Pharaoh's hand. Joseph told the butler that within three days Pharaoh would forgive him. In three days' time the butler was duly reinstated.

The baker's dream was also of three – three baskets of choice bread carried on his head. In the top basket also was every kind of food he prepared for Pharaoh, but birds were eating it. According to Joseph, in three days' time Pharaoh would hang the baker and the birds would eat his flesh. And so it happened.

Two years later, Pharaoh had a dream. Standing by the Nile he saw seven cows, sleek and fat, grazing on the reeds. Then seven other cows came from the river, gaunt and lean, and ate the sleek fat cows. This was followed by a dream in which seven ears of corn, full and ripe, grew on one stalk. Next to them were seven other ears, thin and shriveled. The thin ears swallowed up the full ears. Pharaoh summoned the magicians and sages of Egypt and told them of his dream, but no one could interpret it. The butler remembered Joseph and he was brought before Pharaoh.

Joseph interpreted the dream to mean that there would be seven good agricultural years followed by seven years of famine. He told Pharaoh that a shrewd and intelligent man was needed to put aside part of the harvest from the years of plenty to feed the people during the famine. Pharaoh appointed Joseph, who became a high official in Egypt. The famine duly arrived and Joseph's brothers were sent to Egypt to buy grain. Exactly as his dream had foretold, they bowed low before him.

WHAT DREAMS CAN DO FOR YOU

Dreams are messages from the subconscious mind. The subconscious mind is not limited in the way the rational mind is. It is intuitive, reaching beyond time to embrace past, present, and future. Dreams can show the root cause of illness or events, stimulate latent creativity, and highlight unconscious desires. They reveal a great deal about your state of mind, drawing attention to what is ignored or rejected in the waking state. Dreams can also be a "dress rehearsal" to try out different scenarios. It is possible to ask for a dream to answer a specific query.

DREAM SLEEP

Everyone dreams. Sleep consists of distinct cycles with different brainwave patterns, one of which is associated with dreaming. We all need dream sleep. Without it, we quickly become stressed, leading to a breakdown in mental health. Dreams are believed to be the way we process what happens during the day. By and large, these dreams are quickly forgotten – if remembered at all. But every so often there is a special dream, vivid and immediately recallable, one that haunts the edges of the mind.

Dreams like this have a different purpose. They bring to your attention something that is at the back of your mind, not quite consciously recognized. This may be something of which you are unaware, or of which you do not want to be aware. Dreams may also be intimations of something that is to come. In olden times, such a dream would be eagerly sought. The shaman had secret ways to put him or herself into a dreaming trance. Priests gave potions to induce healing dreams. The most humble peasant had recourse to divinatory dream meanings, which passed down through folklore to the present day.

Sir Joseph Noel Paton's representation of Dante's Dream from the Divine Comedy.

Keep your dream journal close to the bed to jot down dreams as soon as you awake.

KEEPING A DREAM JOURNAL

It is possible to train yourself to remember dreams. Keep a special book as a dream journal. Before you go to sleep, affirm that you will remember your dreams. Then, as soon as you wake up, quietly spend a few moments reviewing your dream(s). Have a pen and your dream journal handy and make notes. When you first begin you usually find you can only remember the odd picture, but as you write it comes back to you. If you have trouble waking up sufficiently to do this, you can always mumble into a tape recorder and transcribe the dream later. You may also like to paint your dream or put it into poetic form.

INTERPRETING A DREAM

Not every dream will have great meaning for you. Many will be "processing dreams," although even these can throw light on what is happening to you on a day-to-day level and they are useful to practice on. Other dreams are deeply symbolic and these tend to stand out as somehow different. If you can recall a dream many years later, it is clearly important

All dreams have separate components which need to be synthesized to reach understanding. When interpreting a dream, look at each individual part separately. The age, sex, and circumstances of the dreamer need to be taken into account, and

TYPES OF DREAMS

Anxiety	Arising out of emotional state
"Dress rehearsal"	Trying out different scenarios
Processing	Going over the events of the day
Factual	Confirmation of something of which you are already aware
Warning	An intimation of danger
Precognitive	Showing something in advance
Creative	The solution to a problem

Dreams may be "processing" events happening on a day-to-day level, or may be deeply symbolic. Such dreams tend to stand out as being different somehow.

many of the symbols can be interpreted at different levels. If you are close to the main component of your dream, events will happen quickly, but if you are far away it will take longer to come about. Remember to keep the interpretation loose; ascribing an arbitrary meaning has no value.

ASKING FOR A SPECIFIC DREAM

It is possible to ask for a dream to illuminate something of concern to you. Before you go to sleep, tell yourself firmly and clearly that you will have a dream that will answer your question and you will remember. Repeat this several times.

Traditional Dream Meanings

"The skillful interpreter of dreams is he who has the faculty of observing resemblances."

ARISTOTLE

While each symbol has its own individual meaning, there are some general guidelines to remember. Death in a dream usually signifies transformation or a fresh start rather than actual death. Objects that are clean and shiny are good omens, dirty or dull ones forecast obstacles. Going up is an indication of improvement or success, while going down indicates reversal of fortune. Upsetting something usually means exactly that. When the dream concerns an illness, it is sensible to have a medical checkup. Relatives with whom you are on good terms often signify advancement in business, while those with whom you are not can indicate setbacks. Some dreams are "dreams of contrary": anger, for instance, can mean reconciliation.

SYMBOL	PROPHETIC MEANING
Abyss/avalanche	Danger
Accident to head	Danger to oneself or father
Accident to right foot	Danger to siblings
Accident to left foot	Danger to employees (or servants)
Accident to right hand	Danger to mother
Accident to left hand	Danger to children
Accused by man	Good news
Accused by woman	Bad news
Actor/actress	Deceit, falseness
Airplane	Ambition, success
Altar	Consolation, joy
Ambulance	Wound, illness
Ambush	Betrayal
Angel	Protection, happiness
Anger	Reconciliation
Applause	Reproach
Baby	Luck in the home
Bag/barrel, empty	Poverty
Bag/barrel, full	Abundance
Ball	Opportunity
Ball rolling	Success delayed
Barking	Beware

SYMBOL	PROPHETIC MEANING
Basement	Anguish/torment
Battle	Illness
Beard, black	Betrayal
Beard, cut	Illness
Beard, fair	Good counsel
Bed, empty	Disappointment
Bed, made	Rest
Bed, unmade	Mistakes
Bees, dead	Loss of money
Bell/birds	Good news
Bicycle	Early success
Birdcage	Slander
Blindness	Deceit/betrayal
Boat	Fortunate journey
Bottle, broken	Quarrel
Bouquet	Disappointment
Bread, brown/stale	Worry
Bread, white/fresh	Good luck coming
Bridge	Happy solution
Burial	Early marriage
Burial (one's own)	Serious illness
Butterfly	Inconstancy

SYMBOL	PROPHETIC MEANING
Cake	Family festivities
Castle	Happy event
Cat	Treason
Cemetery	News of death
Chilblains	Indiscretion
Chocolate	Satisfaction
Clock	Important business
Crab	Separation
Cradle	Hope realized
Crime, witness	Exaggerated fear
Death (one's own)	Good health
Dice	Fatal loss
Dog	Faithful love
Drunkenness	Certain success
Eagle	Prosperity
Eggs	Abundance
Empty cage	Marriage breakup
Eyes, beautiful	Love
Eyes, lost	Death of a relative
Feather	Frivolity
Fire, out	Sorrow
Fireplace, smoking	Quarrel
Fireplace, with fire	Family pleasures
Flag/flame	Success
Flowers, white	Death
Frog	Indiscretion
Gambling	Good if losing, bad if winning
Garden	Pleasant surprise
Hair	Trickery
Hand	Flattery
Hat	Disillusionment
Horse, black	Pleasure following sorrow
Horse, white	Wealth
Hospital	Distress
Jewels	Money
Jewels, imitation	Vanity
Key	Missed appointment
Kiss	Deceit
Labyrinth	Mystery revealed
Ladder	Up, success; down, failure
Lantern	Be prudent
Lawyer	Lawsuit, poverty

SYMBOL	PROPHETIC MEANING
Letter	Neglect of friendship
Lighthouse	Protection
Lion	Powerful adversary
Lock, broken	Theft
Maps	Long journey
Mailman	Letter on way
Mask	Lies
Matches, burning	Success
Moon, full	Delay
Moon, misty	Illness
Mouse	Loss of money lent
Owl	Delay beginning
Pin	Wounded self-esteem
Playing cards	Loss of money
Rainbow	End of troubles
Removal	Change of employment
Ring	Engagement/marriage
Ring, broken	Divorce
Road	Broad, happy life; narrow, deceit
Ruins	Reversal of fortune
Scales	Legal business
Scissors	Quarrel, death of friend
Sea	Calm, happiness; rough, anger.
Shaving	Loss of money
Snake	A grudge against you
Tent	Unforeseen adventure
Thief	False friend
Throne	Change of position
Thunderstorm	Danger threatens
Tomb	Long life
Umbrella	Lasting friendship
Umbrella, found	Valuable connection
Undressing	Lack of foresight
Veil, torn	Secrets revealed
Vomit	Great worry
Wallet	Full, loss of profit; empty, money coming
Wealth	Disillusion
Wedding	Short joy
Weeping	Good news
Window, broken	Theft, dispute
Wine bottle	Happy old age

Psychic Abilities

The abilities commonly described as psychic gifts are simply natural extensions of our intuition.

DAVID LAWSON: YOUR PSYCHIC POTENTIAL

Psychic abilities go beyond normal sensory perception. They access and harness intuition and put you in touch with a level of reality that lies behind physical existence. Time has little meaning in a psychic sense and so psychic gifts can access the future as well as the past.

PSYCHIC POTENTIAL

Everyone has the ability to raise their awareness, to access levels beyond those experienced in everyday life, to utilize extrasensory perception as well as the physical senses of sight, sound, touch, taste, and smell. It is a question of honing the intuition, learning to listen to an inner voice, and paying attention to what lurks at the edge of consciousness.

WHAT PSYCHIC ABILITIES CAN DO FOR YOU

Many professional readers apply their psychic gifts to help others. This is particularly useful if you want an objective focus or if you need advice or information from someone in the family who has passed on – although such advice may be anything but objective! The attitudes and prejudices that

Psychic opening up often begins with a glimpse of the aura around someone's head. It is easier to see if the person stands against a plain background.

people carry over with them after death take a long time to fade, but an "evidential reading" can be most reassuring. This is especially so if you have become stuck in the grief process.

Communication with someone who has passed on may also be useful if you wish to heal a breach or to express feelings that remained unsaid. Clearing unfinished business can be most therapeutic. "Messages" from guides and helpers who can see a little further than our limited earth view can also be helpful and are available through channelers and psychics. As with all oracles, common sense and a flexible interpretation need to be applied.

However, developing your own psychic abilities gives you a source of intuitive guidance that you can rely on – once you have learned to distinguish true guidance from wishful thinking! Accessing your psychic gifts expands the boundaries of your perception and hones your intuition. It is part of your spiritual growth.

THE VARIETIES OF PSYCHIC EXPERIENCE

Psychic information is received in different ways. Just as one person physically hears better than another, or is able to see clearly; so some people hear psychically while others see pictures in their mind's eye.

CLAIRVOYANCE

Many psychics use clairvoyance when making contact with spirits, guides, or helpers. It

Children frequently have innate psychic abilities, but quickly close down when confronted with adult disbelief.

translates as "clear sight." Clairvoyants literally look into the future, or into their client's psyche. Information is passed by way of pictures or symbols. Images can be seen internally as though projected onto a screen inside the head (subjective clairvoyance), or externally as though the picture is projected out 2–3 feet (60–90 cm) in front (objective clairvoyance).

Children are naturally clairvoyant, but quickly learn that what is visible to them is not always apparent to adults, or is assumed to be just a fantasy, and so they switch off their gift. However, clairvoyance can be revived. Learning from an expert is the best way to develop your clairvoyance and bring it under conscious control.

*Giving your beloved a rose
takes on a whole new meaning
when you realize that flowers
hold the imprint of the giver.*

CLAIRSENTIESENCE

Clairsentiesence is the ability to receive or sense things. It is a subtle psychic gift, often operating through the physical body as a "gut feeling." Clairsentiesence can be practiced by holding a flower that has been first held by another person. The flower absorbs impressions and passes them on as subtle feelings.

PSYCHOMETRY

Psychometry is the art of holding an object that belongs to someone and reading off impressions and feelings about that person. It is a useful way to begin developing your psychic gifts, and many of the old-fashioned mediums (those who make contact with people who had passed beyond death) based their work on psychometry.

INNER WISDOM

Learning to tune in to your own inner wisdom is a psychic ability. It is best practiced in quiet, meditative moments away from outside stimuli. If you consciously ask that you will receive only the highest guidance for your own good, you will come to recognize a true communication from your own wisdom.

CLAIRAUDIENCE

Clairaudience is the gift of hearing clearly. Information comes through words, thoughts, and "feelings." It may be received through an inner voice or as a distinct outer voice. Many clairaudients, however, are not aware of having heard anything. They just seem to know something or suddenly have an idea pop into their head.

If you are clairaudient, you may well find that loud and discordant noises bother you. You are acutely aware of other people's noise and of background music, for instance. This is partly because noise interferes with what you are receiving, (even when you are not conscious of this), and also because clairaudients do have particularly sensitive hearing.

This ancient Greek plate shows Aegeus, King of Athens, consulting the Delphic Oracle. She holds bay leaves – whose hallucinogenic qualities may have aided her in parting the mists of time .

TELEPATHY

Telepathy is an extrasensory activity. It is the passing of thoughts, words, pictures, and symbols from one mind to another without verbalizing them. Many people are aware of picking up thoughts that are not theirs.

CHANNELING

In a way, channeling has always been practiced. The Oracle at ancient Delphi channeled information from other planes of reality, as did shamans and seers throughout the ages. At the end of the twentieth century, the phenomenon of "channeling" arose. Some of it purported to channel spirits who had passed beyond death, but other channelers claimed their source was extraterrestrial. Many of the predictions and prophecies that came from channeling were extreme, the channel exercising little restraint over what came through.

If you are hoping to develop channeling, this is best done under the guidance of an experienced teacher who can check where the communication is coming from. If you channel alone, remember to "test the spirits" – question, do not take it for granted. And do not be too quick to pass on the results, or to rely upon them yourself.

AUTOMATIC WRITING

In automatic writing, it feels as though something other than the will of the writer is guiding the pen. It should be done when you are in a quiet, meditative state. The pen should be held loosely above a paper pad.

Sitting quietly in a meditative state enables you to draw your focus inward to listen to inner guidance or to receive messages from other realms.

Sortes

O God! That one might read the book of fate

SHAKESPEARE: HENRY IV, PART II

Sortes is Latin for fate or chance lot. It is a form of divine guidance that uses a passage from a book, usually spiritual or philosophical, to answer a specific question. Sortes provides a fast answer and can be used when it might be inappropriate to lay out other divinatory methods.

WHAT IS SORTES?

Sortes is opening a text at random, putting your finger on the text and then reading off the answer. The Bible is often used but, for people who believe this is disrespectful, philosophical books can be substituted – although the early Christian bishop St. Augustine recommended the use of biblical Sortes in cases of spiritual difficulty. Traditionally, from classical times onward, the works of Virgil, especially the *Aeneid*, are consulted.

Sortes usually gives an answer which is straight and to the point. In M. R. James's *Ghost Stories of an Antiquary* there is an account of a man who received the answer: "Seek ye me in the morning and I shall not be there." In the morning he was found dead. The Roman Emperor, Gordianus

Allow your chosen book to open where it will and, without looking at the text, place your finger on the page. The passage on which your finger lies is your answer.

reigned but a few days. His oracular warning from the *Aeneid* had been: "Fate only showed him this earth, and suffered him not to tarry." King Charles I of England was warned that "evil wars would break out and he would lose his life." He was the king who was deposed and beheaded by Parliament in the English Civil War. A more recent example is that of the British journalist John McCarthy who was held captive in modern-day Lebanon in the 1980s. He heard a commotion one day and feared he would be moved or, worse still, executed. He opened his Bible (the only book he was allowed) at random and read "Open thy doors, Oh Lebanon" (*Zechariah 11*). Later that day he heard that one of his co-captors had been released.

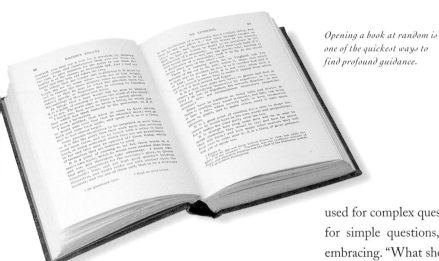

Opening a book at random is one of the quickest ways to find profound guidance.

USING SORTES

Before opening the chosen text, it is usual to focus on the question for a few moments, holding the book between your hands, and to send up a prayer for divine guidance. This prayer can be addressed to a specific deity, or simply to the Universal Guide. Then the book is allowed to fall open where it will. Without looking at the text, simply place your index finger anywhere on the page. The passage indicated is your answer.

You can use an explanatory book from a divinatory pack in the same way without laying out the cards first. The page to which you open the book is the advice or understanding you need. Some people like to pick out a book at random, simply running their hand along a bookshelf until one of the books "falls" out. It is then consulted for guidance. Sortes can even be used with a radio or television – taking the first sentence that is heard after switching on.

WHAT SORTES CAN DO FOR YOU

Sortes is useful when you need specific guidance quickly. While it can be used for complex questions, it is particularly good for simple questions, even when these are all-embracing. "What should I do?" for instance, can be answered by a Sortes text. The secret of success is to choose a book that gives straightforward answers rather than obscure texts that have to be interpreted further or which could be understood in a number of different ways.

SUITABLE TEXTS FOR SORTES

Try: The Bible, *The Lord of the Rings*, James Joyce's *Ulysses*, or any of the works of Shakespeare. Or try the writings of Hermes Trismegistus, Virgil, Plato, Homer, Marcus Aurelius, Ghandi, the Dalai Lama, native teachers, or ancient or modern spiritual advisors. Any book accompanying a divination pack can be used fruitfully.

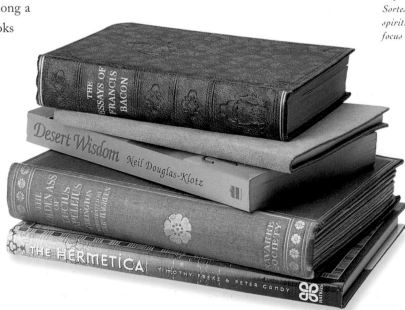

Any book can be used for Sortes, but one with a spiritual or philosophical focus is often the most helpful.

Psychological and Spiritual Insight

If you have eyes to see it, the whole world around you simply reflects your inner mind.

CHUCK SPEZZANO

Modern oracles are guides to the unconscious and to self-discovery. They help you to recognize the part played by the mind in creating everyday reality – and to change it to a better future. They also help you to attune to your spirit and express its creative urge.

GETTING THE MOST FROM THE ORACLES

The packs show you parts of yourself that you may have been hiding from for a long time, whether psychological or spiritual. If your response to a particular card is: "Oh, no, that cannot possibly be right," it is a good indication that this is the very factor that has been eluding you. Much as you may hate the idea, accepting this hidden part of yourself is the key to changing your life.

Inner Child cards can help you to find hidden influences from your childhood and to attune to a childlike part of yourself that has freshness and creativity to offer your adult self, also accessed by the William Blake Tarot *(right).*

So, you need to keep an open and flexible mind, to be able to say: "Well, okay, I'll give it a try. I will act as if it is true and see what develops." If you adhere to this, you can unlock undreamed of potential.

WHAT THE ORACLES CAN DO FOR YOU

You can reawaken your inner child (Inner Child Cards); identify your personal goals, improve your life, work, and relationships (The Enlightenment Pack); find creative inspiration, personal problem-solving, and spiritual self-development (The William Blake Tarot); or explore yourself, the past, present, and future, through the mysterious world of Middle Earth – The Lord of the Rings® Oracle

can be used as a "fun oracle" to provide answers to everyday questions but can also be interpreted at a deep spiritual level.

The Enlightenment Pack is an amazing tool for self-discovery. It offers both "instant answers" to everyday questions and positive, long-term solutions to your biggest challenges. Using the pack helps you to identify and let go of illusions, attachments, outgrown lifescripts, and ingrained family patterns. It provides tools for healing, positive choices, and moving forward. Inner Child Cards gently use the power of childhood fairy tales and mythology to unlock hidden memory. They are excellent for dream work, the recovery process, and for working with children or your own inner child.

The Enlightenment Pack

The Enlightenment Pack reaches into the deepest recesses of your psyche to bring out your fullest potential. It is a powerful guide to self-awareness – an enjoyable process with these delightfully illustrated cards.

The Enlightenment Pack accesses your subconscious mind and brings it out into the light of understanding.

THE CARDS

The cards are a tool for personal growth. They teach personal responsibility, choice, and account-ability. Their creator believes that we can choose to step out of old patterns at any moment. One of the unique factors of The Enlightenment Pack is the concept of choosing "Grace" or asking the Higher Mind to work on your behalf.

The images on the cards are incredibly graphic and have a childlike quality to them that make their meaning instantly recognizable. Divided into six suits and two sets, the cards are color-coded on the back. The first set are Victim, Relationship, and Unconscious, the "trap" or issue cards. The other set are healing cards:

Healing, Gift, and Grace. Victim contains hidden, blocking factors that keep you powerless, without the ability to make life choices. Relationship reveals self-defeating traps that emerge from preexisting family patterns or soul experiences, as described in Unconscious. Soul experiences are expressed through myths and metaphors. They are lessons the soul has come to Earth to learn.

Healing cards transcend traps, remove blocks, and create flow. Gift cards represent gifts that can be chosen instead of traps. Grace cards are a reminder that everything can be accomplished by grace and ease rather than through difficulty and hard work.

USING THE CARDS

You should take as long as you feel you need to attune to these cards. It is useful to remember that the cards reflect how things are in the present moment, but that this can change – indeed choosing for things to be different is a positive tool. You can "choose a miracle." If you pick a negative card, you can ask for a positive solution, and choose a card from Healing, Grace, or Gift to show the way out of your trap, saying: "I choose this over … [the problem]." The cards have been used with thousands of people from all cultures, and they do work. Chuck Spezzano, creator of

An underlying fear may need to be released before success can be achieved. The gift of holiness (or wholeness) is available.

RELATIONSHIP READING

1 What is on your mind

4 What is on your partner's mind

2 What is in your heart

5 What is in your partner's heart

3 The issue in your sexual center

6 The issue in your partner's sexual center

SOUL READING

3 Guilt / Forgiveness

2 Rejection / Acceptance

4 Expectations / Letting go

1 Fears, Loss / Understanding

10 How you see yourself

5 Control / Trust

9 The shadow / Awakening

6 Dead zone / Ease

8 Vision blocks / Creativity

7 Blocks / Gifts

the pack, stresses that you need to make a deliberate choice that you want the cards to succeed, you must have the desire for a breakthrough, and expect a miracle to occur. It may seem unbelievable, but if you believe it happens!

Sometimes you will use the full deck, at others you select from the sets. When you pick a card, do so with your eyes closed so that you will not be influenced by the color coding on the back. One of the quickest and most powerful ways of using the cards is to pick one card at random to represent what is happening to you at this moment. It never fails to clarify the situation.

LAYOUTS

Particularly useful spreads are the Relationship spread, and the "Soul Reading," which describes the healing challenges and gifts you bring into stages of your growth. Both of these use the full deck.

You can also choose three cards – one for the fear or lesson underlying a situation, one for the way forward, and a third for the healing, grace, or gift that will change it.

Inner Child Cards

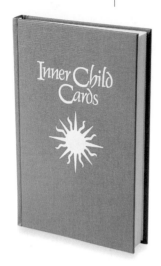

Inner Child Cards reawaken the child in everyone by gently reconnecting with potent archetypes from the inner world. They draw on universal fairy tales, myths, and fables to open hearts and minds to new revelations on the journey of self-discovery.

Storytelling and myth are an integral part of the Inner Child Cards.

THE CARDS

Adapted from Tarot cards, Inner Child Cards can be used for dream work, the recovery process, and working with children, as well as for divining the unconscious forces that motivate your life, and for making a spiritual reconnection. The cards map the soul's journey. Both the Major and Minor Arcana have been refashioned. The twenty-two cards of the Major Arcana represent the great journey of the human soul on its path of destiny, the fifty-six cards of the Minor Arcana the various experiences of the human being within the four worlds of life on planet Earth.

The beautifully illustrated cards draw on fantasy and use universal archetypes in stories and myths to explore the journey of the Divine Child. They highlight hidden lessons within stories such as Sleeping Beauty: Its death and rebirth motif correlating with the Death card of the Tarot. The cards are intended to help you reconnect to your own inner child, healing her or him where necessary.

USING THE CARDS

The cards are designed to be used by free association, as well as with the interpretations provided. So, if a card reminds you of someone

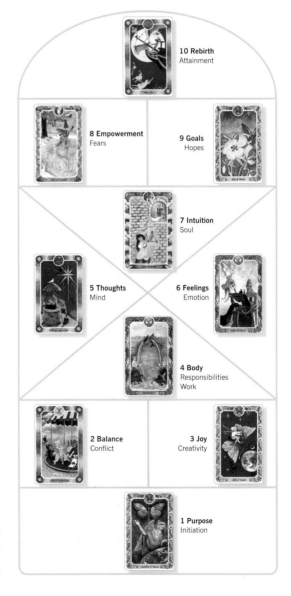

10 Rebirth
Attainment

8 Empowerment
Fears

9 Goals
Hopes

7 Intuition
Soul

5 Thoughts
Mind

6 Feelings
Emotion

4 Body
Responsibilities
Work

2 Balance
Conflict

3 Joy
Creativity

1 Purpose
Initiation

you know, that is a valid connection which it is important to honor. You can weave the qualities of that person into your reading. You can also weave an entire story from your selected cards. The more you play with the Inner Child Cards, the more powerful your intuition will become. The deck is a psychic mirror for your inner self and changing reality.

Shuffle the cards and fan them out face down. Use your left hand to select one (unless you are left-handed, in which case, use your right hand). All cards are read upright.

THE WISHING WELL

Shuffle the cards and fan them clockwise into a large circle. Select one card and place it at the center of the well (i.e. in the middle). This layout answers a particular question or plumbs the depth of your soul.

HOPSCOTCH

The game of hopscotch (far left) equates to the Tree of Life in the Hebrew Kabbala. It reveals the physical, emotional, mental, and spiritual universes in which you reside.

Inner Child Cards are adapted from Tarot cards. The illustrations on the cards draw on fantasy.

THE MAJOR ARCANA

0	Little Red Cap	The Child Within
1	Aladdin and the Magic Lamp	The Creative Child
II	Fairy Godmother	Wisdom Keeper
III	Mother Goose	Mother
IV	The Emperor's New Clothes	Father
V	The Wizard	Initiator
VI	Hansel and Gretel	Physical Union
VII	Peter Pan	Emotional Union
VIII	Beauty and the Beast	Mental Union
IX	Snow White	Spiritual Union
X	Alice in Wonderland	Wheel of Life
XI	The Midas Touch	Cosmic Balance
XII	Jack and the Beanstalk	Sacrifice (making sacred)
XIII	Sleeping Beauty	Death/Sleep
XIV	The Guardian Angel	Protection (Higher Self)
XV	The Big Bad Wolf	Shadow Self
XVI	Rapunzel	Purging
XVII	Wishing upon a Star	The Soul Within
XVIII	Cinderella	Dreams/Visions
XIX	The Yellow Brick Road	The Cosmic Self
XX	The Three Little Pigs	Call to Rebirth
XXI	The Earth Child	Gestating Child

THE MINOR ARCANA

Magic Wands

Art, creativity, intuition, and all that is magical within the realm of nature. They open to joy and passion.

The Swords of Truth

The ego's contradictions in the mental realm and the ability to cut through illusion and false ideologies. They protect, destroy, or conquer, and throw light on mental processes.

Winged Hearts

Feminine, receptive qualities; feelings, emotions, and dreams. They link to unconditional love.

Earth Crystals

The physical plane, money, and security. They teach you how to handle abundance.

William Blake Tarot

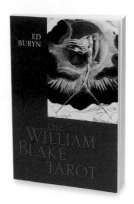

This is the Tarot of the Creative Imagination. It explores the mystical vision and artistry of William Blake, correlating his imagery with traditional Tarot. It is a powerful tool for creative inspiration, personal problem-solving, and spiritual self-development.

FOURFOLD VISION

The Fourfold vision spread is a general purpose one that takes you to the root of matters, focusing your vision.

Mundane experience or situation

0 The problem or issue

4 Seeing through God's eye
Mystical perspective.
Potential experience.

3 Seeing creatively
Thought in emotional form.
Values

2 Seeing though the eye
Personified image.
The mind's eye

1 Seeing with the eye
The facts before you.
One-dimensional

WILLIAM BLAKE

Born in eighteenth-century England, William Blake was a man of liberated ideas and penetrating social vision. Much of his work is mystical and intuitive, rendering it somewhat inaccessible. He invented a pantheon of characters – mythological, supernatural, and historical – who symbolize and enact the human spiritual journey. His complex philosophical system reflects modern psychology and addresses contemporary issues, seeking to liberate the soul. The William Blake Tarot presents his ideas in a way that is easy to absorb and practical to use.

THE CARDS

These beautifully illustrated cards provide a striking introduction to Blake's thought and mythology. Incorporating pictures from his *Illustration of the Book of Job*, the cards kindle the imagination through four Creative Process suits: Painting, Science, Music, and Poetry. They map the soul's journey through Eternity and Triumphs cards.

Triumphs equate to the Major Arcana and are divided into three cycles: Matter, Awakening, and Spirit. The Creative Process suits correlate to the Minor Arcana. In addition there is the Eternity card, representing humankind's hope for divine spiritual consciousness and for living in a world of shining imagination and everlasting truth. Receiving this auspicious card in a reading is a "wake-up call." You need the book with the cards to appreciate the intricacies of this complex system but the cards evoke an immediate response and can be used solely on an intuitive basis if preferred.

Lord of the Rings® Oracle

Based on Tolkien's The Lord of the Rings® *this mystical pack can be used as a practical oracle or as a journey into yourself. It comprises Middle Earth cards, a map, and a ring for revelation and divination. The three parts can be used together or independently.*

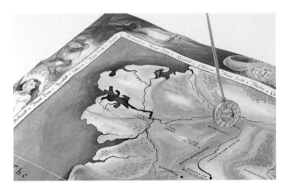

AN INTRODUCTION TO THE ORACLE

The map shows various realms. This landscape represents archetypal scenarios through which we must pass. It is your entire life. All that has happened in the past, all that is happening now, and anything that could possibly lie ahead are shown in symbolic form.

The cards are filters through which you will interact with the influences your life's journey brings. Spread on the map, the cards show decisions you have made, their effects on you and on others, and your possible choices.

The Great Ring can be used as a pendulum for yes-or-no answers. It works by linking to the Universal Mind – a kind of psychic Internet. The ring represents secret

power, but it releases its power in accordance with the inherent potential of its user. It also shows the dangers of using power unwisely. It symbolizes initiation into the mysteries and realities of life.

THE CARDS

The imaginatively illustrated cards take you into Middle Earth to connect with its powerful archetypes. There are forty cards representing scenes and characters from the books. They show you the sum total of all that you are. In the interpretive text, three levels of meaning are given: Esoteric, personal, and reversed. The cards can be used individually to answer questions or they can be laid in spreads.

USING THE ORACLE

There are several ways to use this oracle. For instance, you can cast the ring onto the map. Where it falls will give you a hint as to where to find the answer you seek. Laying out cards will give you further information. You can also use the ring, suspended from a cord, as a pendulum to work with individual cards, refining the information they give you still further.

If swinging the ring over the map, Rivendell would suggest a need to consult with others. The cards would then give deeper guidance as to conduct and outcome. The Shire (bottom left) indicates that your ancestors hold the key – Galadriel success.

Further Reading

The Zodiac Pack, JUDY HALL *Findhorn Press: Scotland 1996.*

Astro-dice, *The Wessex Astrologer, Bournemouth 1989.*

Card Fortune Telling, CHARLES THORP
Foulshams: Cippenham, 1989.

A Company of Angels, DAVID LAWSON
Findhorn Press: Scotland 1998.

The Life You Were Born to Live, DAN MILLMAN
H J Kramer: Tiburon, C.A. 1993.

Chinese Astrology, MAN-HO KWOK *Charles E. Tuttle: Boston 1997.*

The Rune Oracle, JANET THOMPSON *Artomatic: London 2000.*

I Ching: THE BOOK OF CHANGE, *John Blofeld Arkana: N.Y. 1991.*

The Illustrated Guide to Astrology, JUDY HALL *Sterling, N.Y. 1999.*

The Illustrated Guide to Tarot, NAOMI OZANIEC
Godsfield Press: New Alresford 1999.

Your Psychic Potential, DAVID LAWSON *Thorsons: London 1997.*

Celtic Wisdom, CAITLIN MATTHEWS *Thorsons: London 1999.*

The Greenwood Tarot, MARK RYAN & CHESCA POTTER
Sacred Sight: Witney, Oxon 1998.

The Arthurian Tarot, CAITLIN MATTHEWS & JOHN MATTHEWS
Thorsons: London 1995.

The Lords of the Rings Oracle, TERRY DONALDSON
Thorsons: London 1998.

The William Blake Tarot, ED BURYN *HarperCollins: London 1995.*

The Prediction Tarot Pack, SASHA FENTON *Thorsons: London 1985.*

The Angels Tarot, Rosemary ELLEN GULLEY & ROBERT MICHAEL
PLACE *HarperSanFrancisco: C.A. 1995*

The Zen Koan Card Pack, TIMOTHY FREKE *Thorsons: London 1997.*

The Mandala Astrological Tarot, A.T. MANN
Thorsons: London 1997.

Sacred Path Cards, JAMI SAMS *HarperSanFrancisco: C.A. 1990.*

Inner Child Cards, ISHA LERNER & MARK LERNER
Bear & Co: Santa Fe, N.M. 1992.

The Medicine Pack, JAMI SAMS & DAVID CARSON *Bear & Co: Santa Fe, N.M. 1989.*

The Mayan Oracle, ARIEL SPILSBURY & MICHAEL BRYNER
Bear & Co: Santa Fe, N.M. 1992.

Angel Blessings, KIMBERLY MAROONEY
Merrill-West Publishing: Carmel, C.A. 1995.

Voyager Tarot, JAMES WANLESS
Merrill-West Publishing:Carmel, C.A. 1984.

The Eye of Horus: An Oracle of Ancient Egypt, DAVID LAWSON
St. Martins Press: N.Y. 1996.

The Book of Runes, RALPH BLUM *Headline: London 1993.*

The Visual I Ching, OLIVER PERROTTET
Brockhampton Press: London 1996.

The Fortune Tellers Mah Jongg, DEREK WALTERS
Penguin: N.Y. 1985.

The Celtic Tree Oracle, LIZ & COLIN MURRAY
St. Martin's Press: N.Y. 1996.

The Way of Cartouche, MURRY HOPE
St. Martin's Press: N.Y. 1985

The Enchanted Tarot, AMY ZERNER & MONTE FARBER
St. Martin's Press: N.Y. 1990.

The Lover's Tarot, Jane Lyle *St. Martin's Press: N.Y. 1992.*

The Renaissance Tarot, *Simon & Schuster: Fireside N.Y. 1998*

White Eagle Medicine Wheel, WA-NA-NEE-CHE,
WITH ELIANA HARVEY *Connections; Eddison Sadd: 1997.*

The Oracle of the Dreamtime, DONNI HAKASON
Eddison Sadd: 1998.

The Crystal Wisdom Kit, Crystal Love and Crystal Abundance
STEPHANIE HARRISON & BARBARA KLEINER
Piatkus; Eddison Sadd: London 1997.

The Aleister Crowley Pack SAMUEL WEISER: *Maine, USA 1974.*

The Book of Thoth SAMUEL WEISER: *Maine, USA 1974*

The Enlightenment Pack, CHUCK SPEZZANO *Rider: London 1996.*

The Celtic Shaman's Pack, JOHN MATTHEWS
Element: Shaftesbury 1995

The Angel's Script, THEOLYN CORTEN & WILL SHAMAN
Caer Sidi Publications: Witney, Oxon 1997

Angelic Messenger Cards, MEREDITH L. YOUNG-SOWERS
Stillpoint Publishing: Walpole N.H. 1993.

The Crystal Ally Pack, NAISHA AHSIAN
Heaven & Earth Publishing: Heaven and Earth Mashfield Ver. 1996.

The Mythic Tarot, LIZ GREENE *Simon & Schuster: Fireside N.Y. 1987*

Flower Insight Cards, IAN WHITE,
PO Box 531, Spit Junction
NSW 2088 Australia [email:*info@ausflowers.com.au*]

Index

Index